RUDOLF STEINER (1861–1925) called his spiritual philosophy 'anthroposophy', meaning 'wisdom of the human being'. As a highly developed seer, he based his work on direct knowledge and perception of spiritual dimensions. He initiated a modern and universal 'science of spirit', accessible to anyone willing to exercise clear and unprejudiced thinking.

From his spiritual investigations Steiner provided suggestions for the renewal of many activities, including education (both general and special), agriculture, medicine, economics, architecture, science, philosophy, religion and the arts. Today there are thousands of schools, clinics, farms and other organizations involved in practical work based on his principles. His many published works feature his research into the spiritual nature of the human being, the evolution of the world and humanity, and methods of personal development. Steiner wrote some 30 books and delivered over 6,000 lectures across Europe. In 1924 he founded the General Anthroposophical Society, which today has branches throughout the world

Nature Spirits

Selected lectures by
Rudolf Steiner

RUDOLF STEINER PRESS

Compiled and edited by Wolf-Ulrich Klünker

Rudolf Steiner Press
Hillside House, The Square
Forest Row, RH18 5ES

www.rudolfsteinerpress.com

Published by Rudolf Steiner Press 1995
Reprinted 2000, 2003, 2007

Originally published in German under the title *Geistige Wesen in der Natur* by Verlag Freies Geistesleben, Stuttgart, in 1992

A catalogue record for this book is available from the British Library

ISBN 978 185584 018 8

Cover by Andrew Morgan
Typeset by Imprint Publicity Service, Crawley Down, Sussex
Printed and bound in Great Britain by Cromwell Press Limited,
White Horse Business Park, Trowbridge, Wiltshire BA14 0XB

Contents

Introduction

by Wolf-Ulrich Klünker

HUMAN BEINGS stand in a particular relationship to the spiritual world: we live upon the earth; through our physical body and its sense-organs we connect directly with the physical world. As a being of spirit a human being can develop a connection with the spiritual world. This spiritual world is composed of various, differentiated regions; it spans many levels, from the lowest, that of the angel beings, right up to the highest domain of the Holy Trinity. Inasmuch as the human being is a perceiving, discerning spiritual being, he is in direct relationship to angelic beings; the angels, who represent the lower order of the Third Hierarchy, can be seen as intermediaries between the spiritual world and human beings. Whenever a human being turns his attention and recognition to the angel being, he gains access to that domain of reality which is wholly spiritual.

With the other side of his nature a human being partakes of earthly things. These consist of the world of the elements, of the animal kingdom, the plant and mineral worlds. One can perceive these realms as the living forms of nature spirits, who exist in a lower domain than human beings whereas the angels reside above the human sphere. Just as the angels embody, for human beings, a transition or mediation with the spiritual world, so do human beings border upon the domain of nature beings. We can give them an orientation towards the world of spirit, standing as we do between the kingdoms of nature and the realms of spiritual reality.

A human being connects with both nature and spirit; he unites them as one being within himself. This special place in the cosmos has, through the ages, been perceived in Christian tradition and considered as the human being's particular task. In the ninth century, Johannes Scotus Erigena spoke of this task in his *Homelia*, describing human beings as the 'third world' in which are united the 'first world' of spiritual beings and the 'second world' of bodily existence: 'The third world possesses an intermediary nature, uniting the higher spiritual and the lower bodily worlds, making one out of the two; it is in a human being that all creation is united. The human being consists of body and soul. He unites the body of this world with the soul of the other world and so makes one glorious creation. And the body, of course, possesses the whole bodily nature, while the soul possesses the whole non-physical nature. Inasmuch as these natures are united as one, they form the all-encompassing worldly splendour of mankind. That is why the human being is named "everything", for all creation is united in him as in a workshop.'[1] By 'soul' (*anima*), Erigena understands the spiritual essence of the human being; this is clear from the passage in which he describes the soul as possessing 'the whole non-physical nature'. In his analogy to a 'workshop', Erigena suggests that the binding together of two domains within the human being cannot happen by itself, but must be made and worked at.

We can see, then, that human beings have a certain mediating task in regard to nature and the beings inhabiting it. This task of establishing a connection between the kingdom of nature and the spiritual world is not compatible with our having a one-sided exploitative relationship to nature. It also excludes an investigation of nature beings which is fired only by curiosity and a desire for knowledge. A human being cannot really involve himself with these beings simply in order to satisfy his curiosity. The aim of his striving for knowledge about them must, rather, be to create a connection between the worlds of nature and spirit: in other words to establish a connection between nature beings and angel beings. Only a human being can make this connection, for he alone unites both realms within himself. If he withdraws from this task, both realms remain separate.

The perception and understanding of nature spirits or elemental beings is essentially connected with a task which one can call 'cosmic', an evolutionary task which only human beings can accomplish, because of their special position within the cosmos. That is why the question about elemental beings is intimately bound up with the whole cosmos and its evolution, as expressed in the traditions of Christianity.

Knowledge and Nature Beings

We see, then, that a perception of, and understanding for, elemental beings is integral to our consciousness of our task in cosmic evolution. Rudolf Steiner points to the need for such a consciousness when, in a lecture, he formulates the question: 'Can we, as human beings, do something for these elemental spirits?... Can we do anything to free them from their state of enchantment?'[2] He answers this question by differentiating between nature-investigation of two kinds. A human being can, in the first case, remain 'a mere observer of the material phenomena which come towards him. If this is so, the elemental spirits enter him, sit there inside him and have gained nothing from the world-process except that they have come in to him from the outer world.' The other form of observation is practised by one who 'digests his impressions spiritually by thinking about them, and by forming concepts about the underlying spiritual foundation of the world. That is, a person who does not merely stare, but ponders over its nature; a person who feels the beauty of things and ennobles his impressions.' The elemental beings can be released from their 'enchantment' and made free to reassume their original destiny according to the degree to which we develop a spiritual relationship to nature. 'As a result of this spiritual activity he redeems the elemental being that streams toward him from the outer world, thus raising it to its previous state. He releases the elemental being from its enchantment. So, through our spiritual activity, we can release beings who are bewitched in air, water and earth...' Mankind's task therefore consists in developing a particular attitude of mind towards the world.

Human beings can work at the freeing of other kinds of elemental being when they create in themselves a certain attitude of *soul*, which Rudolf Steiner describes as 'industrious and reproductive': 'When a person is lazy, these elementals continually flow into him unchanged. Through his idleness he leaves unchanged those elemental beings who are chained to darkness at night. Those elemental beings who enter into him when he is active and industrious are led back into the daylight.'

Human beings can also develop a third kind of attitude, an attitude of *life*, and thereby release yet another form of elemental being: 'A person who is bright and cheerful, who is satisfied with life, who is of a cheerful disposition because of his understanding of the world is continually liberating beings who are chained because of the waning moon. These beings enter into him but are continually released because of his serene soul disposition, his inner contentment, his harmonious view of life.' One can easily imagine that the development of such an attitude of *life* has a stronger transformative effect upon a human being than is produced by the attitudes of *soul* and *mind*. It becomes clear that a recognition of the elemental beings is inevitably bound up with mankind's own further evolution. This evolution begins with an attitude of mind, passes through a mood of soul and leads to a profound attitude towards life.

Ultimately human beings can take a further step in inner development and thereby free a fourth kind of elemental being: 'Let us take a person who, with the approach of Christmas, carries an ever greater feeling of devotion in his heart, one who understands the true meaning of this festival, which is that as outer nature dies the spirit must be all the more awake. Let us assume such a person lives through the winter season and at Easter realizes that the time of sleep for the spirit is connected with the enlivening processes in nature. He then experiences the Easter festival with understanding.'

Rudolf Steiner describes the capacity that is thus developed as 'religious understanding for natural processes', as distinct from a 'merely outer religion.' This *religious* attitude consists in a striving to create an *inner* context and connection, which is not immediately evident in outer nature. The example chosen here by Rudolf Steiner refers to the seasons of the year, yet it also holds good in other contexts. Through his consciousness a human being inwardly complements, rounds out to wholeness, what is not immediately apparent in nature. In this way a stage of development is attained in which he not only engages himself in inner *reaction*, as in the first three stages, but also complements, or one could say *creates*, a missing aspect of nature. In order to do this, he must have learnt to grasp a whole context, must allow it to live in him and recognize in each case what is not present in nature, so that he can add, from his spiritual life, what is lacking. The principle, which could be summed up as 'intentional inner activity in contrast to mere observation', comes here to a very significant culmination.

There exists a strange connection between the elements and human knowledge. In Rudolf Steiner's fourth Mystery Drama, it becomes clear that the human soul can either lift itself up to the spirit and so to its own essence, or alternatively can, as it were, remain 'possessed' by elemental realities:

> The conflicts of the elements have blown
> Away her error's fabric of appearance;
> Which now lives on within the elements' fury.
> Only her essence has the soul preserved.[3]

What is expressed in these lines is that the part of the soul which is bound up with illusion and appearance has, as it were, been absorbed by the elements. The essence or being of the soul itself, however, has risen up to the spirit. The step, here described as the goal of an ancient Egyptian initiation, could not in this case be completed by the one being initiated. If he had truly achieved recognition and understanding his soul would have found itself in the Spirit-Self. But it was unable to pass through a process of self-knowledge, giving itself over instead to the weaving of the elements. Therefore it created 'being' rather than knowledge and entered into a non-spiritual, elemental form of existence. The neophyte should, instead of directly experiencing the elemental world, have permeated it with knowledge and understanding. It becomes apparent after the neophyte's awakening that he has connected himself with the elements and lived within them, instead of gaining understanding about them. Therefore the life of the elements has taken the place of a process of knowledge. In the cultural epoch referred to here, initiation consisted in recognition of the movements of elemental powers, not in becoming them. But this would only have been possible, at that time, if the one to be initiated had meditated on a 'word' which the initiating priest had given to him, which was intended to have a spiritual effect.[4] In those days one could be protected from being absorbed into elemental life by the thought-forms of someone else; in our time this would have to occur through one's own understanding and knowledge.

A similar set of circumstances is portrayed – again in the fourth Mystery Drama – which also has significance for the present day. A condition of soul from one's own past, which has been overcome, enters the realms of the elements when it is no longer appropriate or relevant to one's present stage of biographical development. Yet it can still be apparent in the experiencing of oneself, 'shadowing forth from outlived times'. The past which appears in this way

> ...constrains you not, for you can rule it.
> Compare it with the elemental beings,
> With shades and shadows of all kinds,
> Place it also in the sphere of demons;
> Then you will recognise its true extent.
> But seek your own self in the realm of spirit...[5]

In this context, the elemental nature appears as the soul-residue of the past. We are not controlled by it if we can confront it with conscious recognition. We must not confuse it with ourself but must, rather, separate it from ourself, objectify it. Then we can discover 'its true extent'. Real self-knowledge does not begin with the elemental forces of one's own past state of soul, but 'in the realm of spirit', in other words, with the soul's future, with the spirit towards which the soul is evolving. This allows the soul's outlived past to unite itself with the elements

> Which work unconsciously through world-expanses
> Eluding constantly the soul's wakefulness.[6]

The old forces of soul unite with the elements; from the purified soul of the present arises spirit. The world of the elements appears, in this context, as outmoded powers of soul, which have a demonic influence when they encroach on the present, but which we can lead back into the unconsciousness of elemental existence and so be rendered harmless. We are able to do this when we journey upon a path of spiritual development. The relationship between elemental world, human soul and spiritual reality is therefore also one of time: the soul evolves towards spirit (that is, into the future); when this evolution does not take place, then old soul forces (the soul's past) condense into elemental existence.

The elemental world borders directly on the soul-world of human beings and can be influenced by processes of thought and understanding. What was described above in connection with outer nature is also valid in the realm of self-knowledge: an understanding for the elemental world is only possible when it is sought, not through simple, passive observation but through an engaged and intentionally directed activity of enquiry. This activity can also be described as a *moral* quality which, in the realm of self-knowledge, consists of being clearly focused on the possibilities for one's own future development. Such an activity must, in contrast to a holding fast to past soul-states, be consistently and intentionally upheld.

It is for this reason that a true recognition of the elemental world always contains a moral aspect; without it, human beings are imprisoned in elemental reality. By 'moral' is meant (in accord with a philosophy of idealism) a disposition of will which we continually draw out of ourselves anew and must consciously uphold. If this does not occur, the human 'I' succumbs to the elemental powers. 'One cannot develop a sense of oneself in the elemental world without strenuously exercising one's power of will, without willing oneself. That, however, requires the over-coming of the human love of comfort, which is enormously deep-rooted.'[7] 'One must experience the great significance of the fact that, at the moment in which one is no longer strong enough to activate not the thought but the power of will involved in saying 'I will myself', one has the sensation of fainting away. To fail to hold oneself up in the elemental world means to fall, as it were, into a faint.'

The uniting of perception and morality is also necessary for an understanding of the elemental world, because perception unsustained by moral activity is open to great illusions in this realm of reality. Both the 'I'-experience and an insight into the 'object realm' of the elements need to be permeated with intentional thinking activity. 'Inner courage and firmness of purpose must, above all things, be developed in the soul; a weak purpose weakens the whole soul-life and a weak soul-life draws one into the elemental world. That should not be, if one wishes to live rightly and truly within the elemental world. It is for this reason that no one who truly takes experiences of higher worlds seriously will ever fail to emphasize that in order to strengthen soul-life, so that it can rightly enter into higher worlds, one must also strengthen the moral powers of the soul.'

A Perspective on the Historical and Spiritual Evolution of Christianity

A very similar connection between knowledge and the elemental world can be found in the previously cited *Homelia* by Johannes Scotus Erigena: 'The Holy Scriptures are ... like a spiritual world, composed of four parts, as though of the four elements. Their "earth" occupies a middle and lower position – similar to a central point – in the form of history. Around it flows the cascade of moral understanding, commonly termed "ethics" by the Greeks, which is comparable to the waters of the earth. Around both history and ethics streams, as around the two lower realms of earth and water, the air and atmosphere of *natural science*, which the Greeks name "physics". Beyond and around all these is spread the ethereal, blazing globe of the fiery heavens, that is, the loftiest perception of the nature of God, which the Greeks refer to as "theology".'[8]

Erigena here relates four domains of elemental reality to four realms of knowledge. An historical understanding, called 'history' by Erigena, is connected by him to the earth, a moral understanding to water, a knowledge of nature to the air and a theological enquiry into purely spiritual truths, to fire. One must bear in mind that Erigena did not intend a simple outward comparison; this passage is, rather, to be understood as an indication of the inner connection which was still experienced in the ninth century between the elemental world and human knowledge. It is interesting to notice that Erigena has an understanding of 'natural science' which is unusual in our day: he places it, not in relation to the earth but higher than ethics, immediately below a perception of purely spiritual reality ('theology'). His introductory remark referring to the Holy Scriptures as a kind of 'spiritual world' makes clear that Erigena sees the spiritual world as being composed of various realms in a way similar to the differentiation of the physical world into its constituent elements. Knowledge of the elements and spiritual knowledge have stages which relate to each other. This insight can provide the means to progress from an understanding of the elements to a recognition of the elemental beings.

Erigena's understanding of nature is, in the context of the spiritual history of Christianity, one of the roots from which Rudolf Steiner's view of the elements arises. In his most important work, *Categories of Nature (De Divisione Naturae)*, Erigena initially develops an overall concept of nature: 'Often have I pondered and carefully investigated to the best of my power how all things which my mind can grasp or which are beyond the reach of its enquiry can first and foremost be divided into that which is and that which is not. And the general term for all this is given to us in the word "nature".'[9] To this definition of nature in its most all-encompassing sense, as what is and what is not, can be added one tiny word, which makes clear what Erigena means: nature is composed of what is and what is not *yet*. In other words, nature consists of what has already developed and what is still in the process of developing. Our modern consciousness mostly sees in nature what already exists, what has already developed; it is extremely difficult to find appropriate ways of perceiving and experiencing what exists as potential in nature, what is still becoming. Nature is most commonly perceived in its products and results, which are accessible to human senses. The potential aspects of nature, on the other hand, cannot be grasped in this way, but can only reveal themselves to different organs of perception. The realm of becoming, potential nature, consists most immediately of the elemental world, which cannot reveal itself to sense-organs but only to organs of soul and spirit.

Elemental reality is related, on the one hand then, to sense phenomena. But on the other hand it is also connected with the spiritual world. Erigena gives expression to both connections in the passage which follows: 'It seems to me that there are four divisions of nature. One creates and is not created; then there is one which is both created and creates; the third kind is created but does not create; the fourth neither creates nor is created.'[10] Four realms of reality are referred to here, which arise from the relationship between what creates and what is created. Human beings of the modern age have turned their attention from this relationship to another: nowadays we are more aware of the connections between the physical world and the world of our perceptions. In a lecture given in 1923, Rudolf Steiner undertook a similar division of realms of reality: he distinguishes a first world, which is physical and can be perceived; then a second world, which lies beyond the physical and cannot be perceived; a third world, which lies beyond the physical and can be perceived; and finally a fourth world, which is physical and cannot be perceived.[11]

Erigena's four divisions of nature are not directly parallel to the four realms of reality described by Rudolf Steiner; they are two different perspectives. Erigena ascribes his 'creating and not created' nature to God; his 'creating and created' nature to the causes of things; his 'created and not creating' nature to human beings and the world; and his 'not creating and not created' nature to the end of the world, when all processes of evolution will have come to an end and God will be everywhere in everything. This perspective reflects old Christian traditions in which, for example, there is no clear differentiation between higher spiritual beings (the 'angels' of Christian scriptures) and nature.

Rudolf Steiner, on the other hand, describes the physical world we can perceive as that realm of reality which a human being experiences with a certain immediacy as 'his' world; the realm of reality beyond the physical, which cannot be perceived, is the home of the Third Hierarchy of spiritual beings; the Second Hierarchy resides in the world beyond the physical which can be perceived; the physical world which cannot be perceived is the realm of the First Hierarchy. But in spite of these differences of perspective and content, the views of Erigena and Rudolf Steiner are united across the centuries in their effort to grasp visible and invisible nature as one whole, and make it accessible to human enquiry.

Such is also the way in which one can find access to elemental reality. In Erigena's *Categories of Nature* there appears a connection between human knowledge and elemental reality which is very similar to the one expressed by Rudolf Steiner. Erigena speaks of the physical world 'returning' into the elements, then the elements returning into 'soul', which ultimately evolves into the spiritual 'original causes'. This transition from the physical world into a spiritual reality is placed by Erigena in complete accord with Christian tradition – at the 'end of the world'. In order for us to understand this today, we need to translate his concepts and arguments into contemporary ways of thinking; which means, above all, to unite them with the idea of evolution. Then the traditional Christian views of the end of the world, in which God will be everywhere in everything, can be understood as an old way of trying to unite sense and spiritual worlds. What is, for Erigena, a process of development towards the end of the world can be understood today as a connection between different realms of reality, which can be realized and achieved in the present through knowledge and understanding. Then we can see Erigena's thinking as an attempt to unite physical and spiritual realities by portraying an evolutionary connection between physical, elemental, soul and spiritual reality.[12] Erigena speaks of a transition of physical reality into the four elements (fire, air, water, earth), of a subsequent metamorphosis of elemental reality into soul-existence; and finally he describes a further step: 'A similar journey is made by the soul itself, which elevates itself into spirit, so as to become more glorious and more like God.'[13]

The elemental world is seen by Erigena as a realm of transition between physical and soul-spiritual reality. It becomes obvious from his descriptions that an understanding of the relationship between physical and soul-spiritual worlds is only possible when one takes account of this intermediary realm. Erigena clearly perceives that this transition can be understood as soon as one relinquishes ideas about fixed, constant shapes and forms which are apparent in the physical world: 'The four simple elements of the world are not, after all, enclosed in forms: for they are to be found everywhere in the world, and from no part of the world is their influence absent. And how could that which is everywhere in the world be confined in a firmly encompassed form? Therefore there are corporealities which do not have a form perceptible to the senses.'[14] The elemental world has, in common with soul-spiritual reality, an outward formlessness. If one can grasp this thought, it is not difficult to imagine that in the elements there are elemental beings at work.

Erigena gazes, finally, into a future in which human beings will be the creators of reality; alongside the given or natural world they will have brought forth two out of themselves: 'It will happen, as we have often emphasized, that the blessedness of the just will be elevated *beyond all natural powers* by the grace of the Creator; so also will the justice of the same Creator punish the godless by casting them down *beneath all nature*. For what is lower and deeper beneath all nature than the vanity of all vanities and the false imaginings about things, for these will fade away into oblivion. Therefore there arises the wonderful and inexplicable, which yet will be confirmed by true reason and consideration of the Holy Scriptures; that the just will be blessed *above all natural good* and the impious, on the contrary, will be punished *beneath all natural good*, and that he whose nature partakes of both good and bad will be placed in the middle between these two.'[15] In this passage, two realms are referred to, regions above and below nature, which are created by the human being himself and which, as it were, form a garment around the old, already created nature. The realm below nature is the product of 'vanities' (*vanitates*) and 'false imaginings' (*imaginationes*), in other words, of moral errors and mistakes. One can also conclude that the realm above nature arises from true knowledge, understanding and moral conduct. We can interpret what Erigena expresses in the language of Christian tradition in the following way: the moral constitution of the human being is, as it were, the 'substance' which forms the realm above nature, whereas the failure to develop morality creates a 'negative substance' in the realm below nature. One need only take one small further step in order to unite the view of Erigena with Rudolf Steiner's portrayal, that of the elemental beings finding release through human recognition and morality.

Preparation for the Future

There is, then, a connection between moral development in human beings and the future evolution of nature and the nature beings. By 'moral' is not meant anything at all moralistic but rather a human being's spiritual self-determination, something like the idea of ethics in German idealistic philosophy: a human being takes his own further development in hand when he reaches out beyond his natural and biographical circumstances and sets himself spiritual aims. To the degree that this becomes possible, he becomes free. In so doing, he also contributes to the further evolution of nature. Therefore the future evolution of nature depends upon mankind becoming free. That is the Christian aspect of the human being's relationship to nature. Only when he understands himself to be a developing being and takes his own spiritual development in hand can nature and its beings also develop. It is in this way that the following statement of Rudolf Steiner can be interpreted: 'One can only understand what should truly come about through the Mystery of Golgotha when one can look back and perceive what once occurred naturally, which now needs to occur morally.'[16] This situation is evidently new in the history of mankind and the earth; it is very apparent, for example, in the ecological problems of the last decades. Precisely in this area it has, for the first time, become obvious to what extent the spiritual and moral development of the human being determines the fate of the natural environ-ment. However, ecological questions must be seen only as an initial perspective on much more far-reaching evolutionary steps.

If one examines the understanding of nature expressed in this volume of lectures by Rudolf Steiner, without holding fast to particular concepts, one can discern as a continuous thread three overriding aspects of nature:

1. Past nature (the physical); this appears to human sense perception and has completed its development.
2. Present nature (the etheric); this is still developing and passing continuously into past nature.
3. Future nature (morality which human beings are creating now); its form will depend upon the moral evolution of mankind and will become the nature which will have been created by human beings themselves. It will be prepared upon the earth but will find its ultimate form in the Jupiter stage of future evolution.

Elemental beings are particularly connected with past nature (which however is still present and visible) and with present nature. Human beings will themselves become, in the future, beings who create nature, but who do so through moral self-determination. This process will gradually release the nature beings, through a human knowledge and understanding characterized by engaged activity rather than by a desire to satisfy curiosity. When a human being succeeds in forming, alongside a perception rooted simply in the senses, an active conceptual understanding of created nature, then he can release the spirits who are bound up within it. Human knowledge thus acquires an enormous significance for the evolution of spiritual beings. One can see from this that there is an interdependency between the elemental world in nature, human knowledge and moral development. It is only at this level that one can begin to speak of the etheric aspect of reality. To reach it, human beings must develop new kinds of knowledge, which will be the basis for the creation of a future nature, one which can only be formed through human moral relationships with creative powers which are beyond and above nature.

Rudolf Steiner placed the connection between elemental world, human knowledge and morality in a particular historical context: the development of Aristotelianism from ancient times to the Middle Ages and subsequently to the present day.

In lectures given in the years 1923 and 1924 he repeatedly assigned to anthroposophical spiritual science the task of reuniting the legacy of an Aristotelian understanding of nature with its original impulses.[17] Science and moral understanding should, he affirmed, be joined together; this unity would complete the 'Christianization' of Aristotelianism, which was begun but not fully achieved in the Aristotelian scholasticism of the Middle Ages. Such a process would connect both with the ancient traditions of Aristotelianism as well as with its medieval forms (such as, for example, the works of Thomas Aquinas). This far-reaching task is set us when we try to reach an understanding about spiritual beings in nature or attempt to shed light on the connection between morality, knowledge and science.

This task not only concerns the development of a new kind of scientific knowledge: it is also relevant to our understanding of ourselves and to our future way of life. We can, increasingly, only understand ourselves and our relationship to the cosmos when we recognize ourselves as spiritually evolving beings. This is the point at which all actions guided by nature come to an end for us: moral self-determination replaces what we have brought with us in the form of a natural and biographical past. And this is obviously also the point of human evolution at which such a moral self-determination begins to be significant for the further evolution of spiritual beings in nature.

This quite new state of affairs in the history of mankind is also the historical point at which the development of science and technology began to have a harmful effect upon the natural environment. Rudolf Steiner characterized this moment in mankind's history in the following words: 'In the scientific age, which begins in the middle of the nineteenth century, the activities of human culture not only slide gradually into the lowest realms of nature, but also sink below nature. Technology becomes sub-natural.'[18] This situation presents us with a specific task of knowledge: 'Our age requires a knowledge which goes above and beyond nature, because it must come to terms with the dangerous influence of life which has sunk beneath nature.' Our task is to find 'an inner strength of enquiry', which will enable the human being to 'climb at least as far in spiritual knowledge to what is beyond the earth and above nature, as he has sunk below nature in technology.'[19] An interest and concern for the spiritual beings in nature, which the following lectures should encourage, can be seen as the first step towards a knowledge that is necessary to counteract the dangers that confront us.

I. Elemental Beings of Earth and Water

Helsinki, 3 April 1912

WHEN OUR friends here gave me a warm invitation to come to them, they requested me to speak about the spiritual beings we find in the realms of nature and in the heavenly bodies. Our theme will compel us to touch upon a realm that is very far removed from all the knowledge humanity is given today by the external world, the intellectual world. From the very beginning we shall have to allude to a domain whose reality is denied by the outer world today. I shall take only one thing for granted, namely, that as a result of the studies you have made in spiritual science, you will meet me with a feeling and perception for the spiritual world; in respect to the manner in which we shall name things, we shall come to a mutual understanding in the course of the lectures. All the rest will, in certain respects, come of itself when, as time goes on, we acquire an understanding born of feeling and of perception for the fact that behind our sense world, behind the world which we as human beings experience, there lies a world of spirit, a spiritual world; and that, just as we penetrate into the physical world by regarding it not only as a great unity but as specified into individual plants, animals, minerals, peoples, persons, so we can specify the spiritual world into different classes of individual spiritual beings. So that in spiritual science we do not merely speak of a spiritual world, but of quite definite beings and forces standing behind our physical world.

What, then, do we include in the physical world. First, let us be clear about that. As belonging to the physical world, we reckon all that we can perceive with our senses, see with our eyes, hear with our ears, all that our hands can grasp. Further, we reckon as belonging to the physical world all that we can encompass with our thoughts in so far as these thoughts refer to external perception, to that which the physical world can say to us. In this physical world we must also include all that we, as human beings, do within it. It might easily make us pause and reflect when it is said that all that we, as human beings, do in the physical world forms part of that world, for we must admit that when we act in the physical world we bring down the spiritual into that world. People do not act merely according to the suggestions of physical impulses and passions, but also according to moral principles; our conduct, our actions, are influenced by morals. Certainly when we act morally, spiritual impulses play a part in our actions; but the field of action in which we act morally is, nevertheless, the physical world. Just as in our moral actions there is an interplay of spiritual impulses, even so do spiritual impulses permeate us through colours, sounds, warmth and cold, and through all sense impressions. The spiritual is, in a sense, always hidden from external perception, from that which the external human being knows and can do. It is characteristic of the spiritual that we can only recognize it when we take the trouble, at least to a small extent, to become other than we have been hitherto.

We work together in our groups and gatherings; and not only do we hear there certain truths that tell us that there are various worlds – that the human being consists of various principles or bodies, or whatever we like to call them – but by allowing all this to influence us, although we may not always notice it, our soul will gradually change to something different, even without our going through an esoteric development. What we learn through spiritual science makes our soul different from what it was before. Compare your feelings after you have taken part in the spiritual life of a working group for a few years – the way you feel and think – with the thoughts and feelings you had before, or with the way in which people think and feel who are not interested in spiritual science. Spiritual science does not merely signify the acquisition of knowledge; it signifies most pre-eminently an education, a self -education of our souls. We make ourselves different; we have other interests. When one imbues oneself with spiritual science, the habits of attention for this or that subject which one developed during previous years alter. What was once of interest is of interest no longer; what was of no interest previously now begins to be interesting in the highest degree. We ought not simply to say that only a person who has gone through esoteric development can attain to a connection with the spiritual world; esotericism does not begin with occult development. The moment that, with our whole heart, we make any link with spiritual science, esotericism has already begun; our souls begin at once to be transformed. There then begins in us something resembling what would arise, let us say, in a being who had previously only been able to see light and darkness, and who then, through a special and different organization of the eyes, begins to see colours. The whole world would appear different to such a being. We need only observe it, we need only realize it, and we shall soon see that the whole world begins to have a new aspect when we have for a time gone through the self-education we can get in a spiritual-scientific circle. This self-education to a perception of what lies behind physical facts is a fruit of the spiritual-scientific movement in the world, and is the most important part of spiritual understanding. We should not believe that we can acquire spiritual understanding by mere sentimentality, by simply repeating continually that we wish to permeate all our feelings with love. Other people, if they are good, wish to do that too. This would only be giving way to a sort of pride. Rather, we should make it clear to ourselves how we can educate our feelings – by letting the knowledge of the facts of a higher world influence us and by transforming our souls by means of this knowledge. This special manner of training the soul to a feeling for a higher world is what makes a spiritual scientist. Above all, we need this understanding if we intend to speak about the things that are to be spoken of in the course of these lectures.

One who, with trained occult vision, is able to see behind the physical facts immediately finds – behind all that is spread out as colour, sound, warmth, and cold, behind all that is embodied in the laws of nature – beings that are not revealed to the external senses, to the external intellect, but that lie behind the physical world. Then, as one penetrates further and deeper, one discovers, so to speak, worlds with beings of an ever higher order. If we wish to acquire an understanding of all that lies behind the sense world, then, in accordance with the special task that has been assigned to me here, we must take as our real starting point what we encounter immediately behind the sense world as soon as we raise the very first veil that sense perceptions spread over spiritual happenings. As a matter of fact, the world that reveals itself to trained occult vision as the one lying next to us presents the greatest surprise to contemporary understanding, to our present powers of comprehension. I am speaking to those who have, to some extent, accepted spiritual science. Therefore I may take it for granted that you know that immediately behind what meets us externally as a human being – behind what we see with our eyes, touch with our hands, and grasp with our understanding, in ordinary human anatomy or physiology – behind what we call the physical body – we recognize the first supersensible human principle. This supersensible principle of the human being we call the etheric or life body. Today, we will not speak of still higher principles of human nature, but need only be clear that occult vision is able to see behind the physical body and to find there the etheric or life body. Now, occult vision can do something similar with regard to nature around us. Just as we can investigate a human being occultly to see if there is not something more than the physical body, and then find the etheric body, so too we can look with occult vision at external nature in her colours, forms, sounds, and kingdoms – in the mineral, the plant, the animal, and the human kingdoms, in so far as these meet us physically. We then find that, just as behind the human physical body there is a life body, we can also find a sort of etheric or life body behind the whole of physical nature.

Only there is an immense difference between the etheric body of all of physical nature and that of the human being. When occult vision is directed to the human etheric or life body, it is seen as a unity, as a connected structure, as a single connected form or figure. When occult vision, on the other hand, penetrates all that external nature presents as colour, form, mineral, plant or animal structures, it discovers that in physical nature the etheric body is a plurality – something infinitely multiform. That is the great difference; the human etheric or life body is a single unitary being – while there are many varied and differentiated beings behind physical nature.

Now, I must show you how we arrive at such an assumption as that just made, namely, that behind our physical nature there is an etheric or life body, strictly speaking an etheric or life world – that is, a plurality, a multiplicity of differentiated beings. To express how we can arrive at this I can clothe it in simple words: we are more and more able to recognize the etheric or life world behind physical nature when we begin to have a moral perception of the world lying around us. What is meant by perceiving the whole world morally? What does this imply? First of all looking away from the earth, if we direct our gaze into the ranges of cosmic space, we are met by the blue sky. Suppose we do this on a day in which no cloud, not even the faintest, silver-white cloudlet breaks the azure space of heaven. We look upward into this blue heaven spread out above us – whether we recognize it in the physical sense as something real or not does not matter. The point is the impression that this wide stretch of the blue heavens makes upon us. Suppose that we can yield ourselves up to this blue of the sky, and that we do this with intensity for a long, long time. Imagine that we can do this in such a way that we forget everything else that we know in life and all that is around us. Suppose that we are able for one moment to forget all external impressions, all memories, all cares and troubles of life, and can yield ourselves completely to the single impression of the blue heavens. What I am now saying to you can be experienced by every human soul if only it will fulfil these necessary conditions; what I am telling you can be a common human experience. Suppose a human soul gazes in this way at nothing but the blue of the sky. A certain moment then comes, a moment in which the blue sky ceases to be blue – in which we no longer see anything that can in human language be called blue. If at that moment, when the blue ceases to be blue to us, we turn our attention to our own soul, we shall notice quite a special mood in it. The blue disappears and, as it were, an infinity arises before us, and in this infinity we experience a quite definite mood in our soul. A quite definite feeling, a quite definite perception pours itself into the emptiness which arises where the blue had been before. If we would give a name to this soul perception, to what would soar out there into infinite distances, there is only one word for it: it is a devout feeling in our soul, a feeling of pious devotion to infinity. All the religious feelings in the evolution of humanity have fundamentally a nuance that contains what I have here called pious devotion. The impression has called up a religious feeling, a moral perception. When within our souls the blue has disappeared, a moral perception of the external world springs to life.

Let us now reflect upon another feeling by means of which we can in another way attune ourselves in moral harmony with external nature. When the trees are bursting into leaf and the meadows are filled with green, let us fix our gaze upon the green which in the most varied manner covers the earth or meets us in the trees; and again we will do this in such a way as to forget all the external impressions that can affect our souls, and simply devote ourselves to what in external nature meets us as green. If once more we are so circumstanced that we can yield ourselves to what springs forth as the reality of green, we can carry this so far that the green disappears for us, in the same way that previously the blue as blue disappeared. Here again we cannot say 'a colour is spread out before our sight', but (and I remark expressly that I am telling you of things that each one of us can experience for ourselves if the requisite conditions are fulfilled) the soul has instead a peculiar feeling that can be expressed thus:

'Now I understand what I experience when I think creatively, when a thought springs up in me, when an idea strikes me; I understand this now for the first time. I can only learn this from the bursting forth of the green all around me. I begin to understand the inmost parts of my soul through external nature when the outer natural impression has disappeared and in its place a moral impression is left. The green of the plant tells me how I ought to feel within myself, when my soul is blessed with the power to think thoughts, to cherish ideas.' Here again an external impression of nature is transmuted into a moral feeling.

Or, again, we may look at a wide stretch of white snow. In the same way as in the description just given of the blue of the sky and the green of earth's robe of vegetation, so too can the white of the snow set free within us a moral feeling for all that we call the phenomenon of matter in the world. And if, in contemplation of the white snow mantle, we can forget everything else, and experience the whiteness, and then allow it to disappear, we obtain an understanding of that which fills the earth as substance, as matter. We then feel matter living and weaving in the world. And just as one can transform all external sight impressions into moral perceptions, so too can one transform impressions of sound into moral perceptions. Suppose we listen to a tone and then to its octave, and so attune our souls to this dual sound of a tonic note and its octave that we forget all the rest, eliminate all the rest and completely yield ourselves to these tones. It then comes about at last that, instead of hearing these dual tones, our attention is directed from these and we no longer hear them. Then, again, we find that in our soul a moral feeling is set free. We begin then to have a spiritual understanding of what we experience when a wish lives within us that tries to lead us to something, and then our reason influences our wish. The concord of wish and reason, of thought and desire, as they live in the human soul, is perceived in the tone and its octave.

In like manner we might let the most varied sense perceptions work upon us; we could in this way let all that we perceive in nature through our senses disappear, as it were, so that this sense veil is removed; then moral perceptions of sympathy and antipathy would arise everywhere. If we accustom ourselves in this way to eliminate all that we see with our eyes, or hear with our ears, or that our hands grasp, or that our understanding (which is connected with the brain) comprehends – if we eliminate all that, and accustom ourselves, nevertheless, to stand before the world – then there works within us something deeper than the power of vision of our eyes, or the power of hearing of our ears, or the intellectual power of our brain-thinking. We then confront a deeper being of the external world. Then the immensity of infinity so works upon us that we become imbued with a religious mood. Then the green mantle of plants so works upon us that we feel and perceive in our inner being something spiritually bursting forth into bloom. Then the white robe of snow so works upon us that by it we gain an understanding of what matter, of what substance is in the world; we grasp the world through something deeper within us than we had hitherto brought into play. And therefore in this way we come into touch with something deeper in the world itself. Then, as it were, the external veil of nature is drawn aside, and we enter a world which lies behind this external veil. Just as when we look behind the human physical body we come to the etheric or life body, so in this way we come into a region in which, gradually, manifold beings disclose themselves – those beings that live and work behind the mineral kingdom. The etheric world gradually appears before us, differentiated in its details.

In occult science, what gradually appears before us in the way described has always been called the elemental world; and those spiritual beings we meet with there, and of whom we have spoken, are the elemental spirits that lie hidden behind all that constitutes the physical sense-perceptible world. I have already said that, whereas the human etheric body is a unity, what we perceive as the etheric world of nature is a plurality, a multiplicity. How then can we, since what we perceive is something quite new, find it possible to describe something of what gradually impresses itself upon us from behind external nature? Well, we can do so if by way of comparison we make a connecting link with what is known. In the whole multiplicity that lies behind the physical world, we first find beings that present self-enclosed pictures to occult vision. In order to characterize what we first of all find there I must refer to something already known. We perceive self-enclosed pictures, beings with definite outline, of whom we can say that they can be described according to their form or shape. These beings are one class that we first of all find behind the physical-sense world. A second class of beings that we find there we can only describe if we turn away from what shows itself in set form, with a set figure, and employ the word metamorphosis or transformation. That is the second phenomenon that presents itself to occult vision. Beings that have definite forms belong to the one class; beings that actually change their shape every moment, who, as soon as we meet them and think we have grasped them, immediately change into something else, so that we can only follow them if we make our souls mobile and receptive, such beings belong to the second class. Occult vision actually only finds the first class of beings, those that have quite a definite form, when (starting from such conditions as have already been described) it penetrates into the depths of the earth.

I have said that we must allow all that works on us in the external world to arouse a moral effect, such as has been described. We have brought forward, by way of example, how one can raise the blue of the heavens, the green of the plants, the whiteness of the snow, into moral impressions. Let us now suppose that we penetrate into the inner part of the earth. When, let us say, we associate with miners, we reach the inner portion of the earth, at any rate we enter regions in which we cannot at first so school our eyes that our vision is transformed into a moral impression. But in our feeling we notice warmth, differentiated degrees of warmth. We must first feel the warmth – warmth must be the physical impression of nature when we plunge into the realm of the earth. If we keep in view these differences of warmth, these alternations of temperature, and all that otherwise works on our senses because we are underground, if we allow all this to work upon us, then through thus penetrating into the inner part of the earth and feeling ourselves united with what is active there, we go through a definite experience. If we then disregard everything that produces an impression, if we exert ourselves while down there to feel nothing, not even the differences of warmth which were only for us a preparatory stage, if we try to see nothing, to hear nothing, but to let the impression so affect us that something moral issues from our soul – then there arises before our occult vision those creative nature beings who, for the occultist, are really active in everything belonging to the earth, especially in everything of the nature of metal, and who now present themselves to his imagination, to imaginative knowledge, in sharply defined forms of the most varied kind. If, having had an occult training, and having at the same time a certain love of such things – it is especially important to have this here – we make acquaintance with miners and go down into the mines, and can forget all external impressions when we are down there, we will then feel rising up before our imagination the first class, as it were, of beings that create and weave behind all that is earthy, and especially in all that pertains to metals. I have not yet spoken today of how popular fairy tales and folk legends have made use of all, in a sense, that is actually in existence; I should like first to give you the dry facts that offer themselves to occult vision. For according to the task set me, I must first go to work empirically – that is, I must give an account, first of all, of what we find in the various kingdoms of nature. This is how I understand the topic put before me.

Just as, in occult vision, we perceive in our imagination clearly outlined nature beings, and in this way can have before us beings with settled form, of whom we see outlines that we could sketch, so it is also possible for occult vision to have an impression of other beings standing immediately behind the veil of nature. If, let us say, on a day when the weather conditions are constantly changing, when, for instance, clouds form and rain falls, and when, perhaps, a mist rises from the surface of the earth, if on such a day we yield to such phenomena in the way already described, so that we allow a moral feeling to take the place of a physical one, then we may again have quite a distinct experience. This is especially the case if we devote ourselves to the peculiar play of a body of water tossing in a waterfall and giving out clouds of spray, if we yield ourselves to the forming and dissolving mist and to the watery vapour filling the air and rising like smoke, or when we see the fine rain coming down, or feel a slight drizzle in the air. If we feel all this morally there appears a second class of beings, to whom we can apply the word metamorphosis, transformation. As little as we can paint lightning can we draw this second class of beings. We can only note a shape, present for a moment, and the moment after everything is again changed. Thus there appear to us as the second class of beings, those who are always changing form, for whom we can find an imaginative symbol in the changing formations of clouds.

But as occultists we become acquainted in yet another way with these beings. When we observe the plants as they come forth from the earth in the spring, just when they put forth the first green shoots – not later, when they are getting ready to bear fruit – the occultist perceives that the same beings that he or she discovered in the pulverizing, drifting, gathering vapours are surrounding and bathing the beings of the budding plants. So we can say that when we see the plants springing forth from the earth we see them everywhere bathed by such ever-changing beings as these. Then occult vision feels that what weaves and hovers unseen over the buds of the plants is in some way concerned with what makes the plants push up out of the ground, draw forth from the ground. You see, ordinary physical science recognizes only the growth of the plants, knows only that the plants have an impelling power that forces them up from below. The occultist, however, recognizes more than this in the case of the blossom. The occultist recognizes – around the young sprouting plant – changing, transforming beings who have, as it were, been released from the surrounding space and penetrate downward; they do not, like the physical principle of growth, merely pass from below upward, but come from above downward, and draw forth the plants from the ground. So in spring, when the earth is robing herself in green, to the occultist it is as though nature forces, descending from the universe, draw forth what is within the earth, so that the inner part of the earth may become visible to the outer surrounding world, to the heavens. Something that is in unceasing motion hovers over the plant. It is characteristic that occult vision acquires a feeling that what floats around the plants is the same as what is present in the rarefied water, tossing itself into vapour and rain. That, let us say, is the second class of nature forces and nature beings. In the next lecture we shall pass on to the description of the third and fourth classes, which are much more interesting; and then all this will become clearer. When we set about making observations such as these, which lie so far from present human consciousness, we must always bear in mind that 'all that meets us is physical, but permeated by the spiritual.'

As we have to think of the individual human being as permeated by what appears to occult sight as the etheric body, so must we think of all that is living and weaving in the world as permeated by a multiplicity of spiritual living forces and beings.

The course to be followed in our considerations shall be such that we shall first describe simply the facts that an occultly trained vision can experience in the external world – facts that are evident to us when we look into the depths of the earth or the atmosphere, into what happens in the different realms of nature, and in the heavenly spaces filled by the fixed stars. And only at the end shall we gather the whole together in a kind of theoretical knowledge that is able to enlighten us as to what lies, as spirit, at the foundations of our physical universe and its different realms and kingdoms.

II. Elemental Beings and the Spirits of the Cosmos

Helsinki, 4 April 1912

YESTERDAY I tried first of all to point out the way that leads the human soul to the observation of the spiritual world hidden directly behind our material physical world, and then to draw attention to two classes or categories of spiritual beings, perceptible to occult vision when the veil of the sense world has been drawn aside.

Today, we shall speak of two other forms or categories of nature spirits. The one is disclosed to trained occult sight when we observe the gradual fading and dying of the plant world in late summer or autumn, the dying of nature beings in general. As soon as a plant begins to develop fruit in the blossom, we can allow this fruit to work upon the soul in the manner described in our last lecture. In this way, we receive in our imagination the impression of the spiritual beings concerned with the fading and dying of the beings of nature. We were able to describe yesterday that in spring the plants are, so to speak, drawn out of the earth by certain beings that are subject to perpetual metamorphosis, and likewise we can say that when, for instance, the plants have finished this development, and the time has come for them to fade, other beings then work upon them – beings of whom we cannot even say that they, too, continually change their forms, for, strictly speaking, they have no form of their own at all. They appear flashing up like lightning, like little meteors now flashing up, now disappearing; they really have no definite form, but flit over our earth, flashing and vanishing like little meteors or will-o'-the-wisps.

These beings are primarily connected with the ripening of

everything in the kingdoms of nature; the ripening process comes about because these forces or beings exist. They are only visible to occult vision when it concentrates on the air itself, indeed, on the purest air possible. We have described the second sort of nature beings by saying that to perceive them we must allow falling water, or water condensed into cloud formations, or something of a like character to work upon us. Now air, as free from moisture as possible, played upon by the light and warmth of the sun, must work upon the soul if we are to visualize in our imagination these meteor-like, flashing and disappearing beings that live in air free from moisture and eagerly drink in the light which permeates the air and causes them to flash and shine. These beings then sink down into the plant world or the animal world, and bring about their ripening and maturity. In the very way we approach these beings, we see that they stand in a certain relation to what occultism has always called the elements.

We find what we described in the last lecture as the first class of such beings when we descend into the depths of the earth and penetrate the solid substance of our planet. Our imagination is then confronted with beings of a definite form, and we may call these the nature spirits of solid substance, or the nature spirits of the earth. The second category we then described are to be found in water that collects and disperses, so that we may connect these spiritual beings with what in occultism has always been called the fluid or watery element. In this element they undergo metamorphoses, and at the same time they do the work of drawing forth from the earth everything that grows and sprouts. The flashing, disappearing beings of whom we have just spoken stand not in connection with the watery element but in connection with the element of air, air when it is as free from moisture as possible. Thus we may now speak of nature spirits of earth, water, and of air. There is a fourth category – of such spiritual beings with which occult vision can become familiar. For this, occult vision must wait until a blossom has brought forth fruit and seed, and then observe how the germ gradually grows into a new plant. Only on such an occasion can such a vision be achieved with ease – in other conditions it is difficult to observe this fourth kind of being, for they are the protectors of the germs, of all the seeds in our kingdoms of nature. As guardians these beings carry the seed from one generation of plants or other nature beings to the next. We can observe that these beings, the protectors of the seeds or germs, make it possible that the same beings continually reappear on our earth, and that these beings are brought into contact with the warmth of our planet – with what from early times has been called the element of fire or heat. That is why the forces of the seed are also connected with a certain degree of heat, a certain temperature. If occult vision observes accurately enough, it finds that the necessary transmutation of the warmth of the environment into such heat as is needed by the seed or germ in order to ripen – the changing of lifeless warmth into a living heat – is provided for by these beings. Hence they can also be called the nature spirits of fire, or of heat. So that, to begin with, we have become acquainted with four categories of nature spirits, having a certain relation to what are called the elements of earth, water, air and fire.

It is as though these spiritual beings had their jurisdiction, their territory, in these elements, just as we human beings have as ours the whole planet. Just as the planet earth is our home in the universe, so these beings have their territory in one or another of the elements mentioned. We have already drawn attention to the fact that for our earthly physical world, for the earth as a whole with its various kingdoms of nature, these different beings signify what the etheric body or life body signifies for individual human beings. Only we have said that in the human being this life body is a unity, whereas the etheric body of the earth consists of many, many such nature spirits, which are, moreover, divided into four classes. The living co-operation of these nature spirits is the etheric or life body of the earth. Thus it is not unity but multiplicity, plurality.

If we wish to discern this etheric body of the earth with occult vision, then – as was previously described – we must allow the physical world to influence us morally, thereby drawing aside the veil of the physical world. Then the etheric body of the earth which lies directly behind this veil becomes visible. Now, how is it, when one also draws aside this further veil, described as the etheric body of the earth? We know that behind the etheric body is the astral body, the third principle of the human being – the body that is the bearer of desires, wishes and passions. Thus, if we disregard the higher principles of human nature, we may say that in a human being we have first of all a physical body behind which is an etheric body, and behind that an astral body. It is just the same in external nature. If we draw aside the physical, we certainly come to a plurality. This represents the etheric body of the whole earth, with all its kingdoms of nature. Now, can we also speak of a sort of astral body of the earth, something that, in relation to the whole earth and to all its kingdoms, corresponds to the astral body of a human being? It is certainly not as easy to penetrate to the earth's astral body as to its etheric body. We have seen that we can reach the etheric body if we allow the phenomena of the world to work upon us not merely through sense impressions but morally as well. If we wish, however, to penetrate further, then deeper occult exercises are necessary, such as you will find described in part – in so far as they can be in an open publication – in my book *Knowledge of the Higher Worlds: How is it Achieved?* At a definite point of esoteric or occult development – as you may read there – a person begins to be conscious, even at a time when he or she is usually unconscious, namely, during the time between falling asleep and waking.

We know that the ordinary unconscious condition, the ordinary human condition of sleep, is caused by our leaving our physical and etheric bodies lying in the bed, and by our drawing out our astral bodies and the rest of what belongs to them; but the ordinary person is unconscious when this occurs. If, however, we devote ourselves more and more to those exercises that consist of meditation, concentration, and so on, and further strengthen the slumbering hidden forces of our soul, then we can establish a conscious condition of sleep. In that case, when we have drawn our astral bodies out of our physical and etheric bodies, we are no longer unconscious but have around us, not the physical world, not even the world just described, the world of the nature spirits, but another and still more spiritual world. When, after having freed ourselves from our physical and etheric bodies, the time comes that we feel our consciousness flash up, we then perceive quite a new order of spiritual beings. The next thing that strikes the occult vision thus far trained is that the new spirits we now perceive have, as it were, command over the nature spirits. Let us be quite clear as to how far this is the case. I have told you that those beings – whom we call the nature spirits of water – work especially in the budding and sprouting plant world. Those – that we may call the nature spirits of the air – play their part in late summer and autumn, when the plants prepare to fade and die. Then these meteor-like air spirits sink down over the plant world and saturate themselves, as it were, with the plants, helping them to fade away in their spring and summer forms. The disposition that at one time the spirits of the water and at another the spirits of the air should work in this or that region of the earth changes according to the different regions of the earth – in the northern part of the earth it is naturally quite different from what it is in the south. The task of directing, as it were, the appropriate nature spirits to their activities at the right time is carried out by those spiritual beings whom we learn to know when occult vision is so far trained that, when we have freed ourselves from our physical and etheric bodies, we can still be conscious of our environment. There are spiritual beings, for instance, working in connection with our earth, with our planet earth, who allot the work of the nature spirits to the seasons of the year, and thus bring about the alternations of these seasons for the different regions of the earth, by distributing the work of the nature spirits. These spiritual beings represent what we may call the astral body of the earth. We plunge into this with our own astral bodies at night when we fall asleep. This astral body, consisting of higher spirits that hover around the planet earth and permeate it as a spiritual atmosphere, is united with the earth; and into this spiritual atmosphere our astral bodies plunge during the night. Now, to occult observation, there is a great difference between the first category of nature spirits – the spirits of earth, water, and so on – and those beings that, on the other hand, direct these nature spirits. The nature spirits are occupied in causing the beings of nature to ripen and fade, in bringing life into the whole planetary sphere of the earth. The situation is different with regard to those spiritual beings who, in their totality, can be called the astral body of the earth.

These beings are such that when we can become acquainted with them by means of occult vision, we perceive them as beings connected with our own souls – with our own astral bodies. They exert such an influence upon the human astral body – as also upon the astral bodies of animals – that we cannot speak of a mere life-giving activity; their activity resembles the action of feeling and thought upon our own souls. The nature spirits of water and air can be observed; we may say they are in the environment. But we cannot say of the spiritual beings of whom we are now speaking that they are in our environment; we are in fact always actually united with them, as if poured into them, when we perceive them. We are merged into them, and they speak to us in spirit. It is as though we perceived thoughts and feelings from the environment – impulses of will, sympathy and antipathy come to expression in what these beings cause to flow into us as thoughts, feelings and impulses of will. Thus, in this category of spirits, we see beings already resembling the human soul. If we turn back again to what has been stated, we may say that all sorts of regulations in time – of divisions in the relations of time and space – are also connected with these beings. An old expression has therefore been preserved in occultism for these beings, whom in their totality we recognize as the astral body of the earth, and this in English would be 'spirits of the periods or cycles of time'. Thus not only the seasons of the year and the growing and the fading of the plants but also the regular alternation which, in relation to the planet earth expresses itself in day and night, is brought about by these spirits which are to be classed as belonging to the astral body of the earth. In other words, everything connected with rhythmic return, with rhythmic alternation, with repetitions of happenings in time, is organized by spiritual beings who collectively belong to the astral body of the earth and to whom the name 'spirits of the periods or cycles of time of our planet' is applicable. What the astronomer ascertains by calculation about the cycle of the earth on its axis is perceptible to occult vision, because the occultist knows that these spirits are distributed over the whole earth and are actually the bearers of the forces which rotate the earth on its axis. It is extremely important that one should be aware that in the astral body of the earth is to be found everything connected with the ordinary alternations between the blossoming and withering of plants and also all that is connected with the alternations between day and night – between the various seasons of the year and the various times of the day, and so on. All that happens in this way calls up – in the observer who has progressed so far as to be able to go out of the physical and etheric bodies in the astral body and still remain conscious – an impression of the spiritual beings belonging to the spirits of the cycles of time.

We have now, as it were, drawn aside the second veil, the veil woven of nature spirits. We might say that, when we draw aside the first veil, woven of material physical impressions, we come to the etheric body of the earth, to the nature spirits, and that then we can draw aside a second veil and come to the spirits of the cycles of time, who regulate everything that is subject to rhythmical cycles. Now, we know that what may be called the higher principle of human nature is embedded in our astral body. At first we understand this to be the 'I', embedded in the astral body. We have already said that our astral body plunges into the region of the spirits of the cycles of time, that it is immersed in the surging sea, as it were, of these spirits. But as regards normal consciousness our 'I' is still more asleep than the astral body. One who is developing occultly and progressing esoterically becomes aware of this, because it is in the spiritual world into which one plunges – which consists of the spirits of the cycles of time – that one first learns to penetrate into the perceptions of the astral body. In a certain respect, this perception is really a dangerous factor in esoteric development, for the human astral body is, in itself, a unity but everything in the realm of the spirits of the cycles of time is, fundamentally, multiplicity, plurality. And since, in the way described, we are united with, and immersed in, this plurality, if we are still asleep in our 'I' and yet awake in our astral body, we feel as if we were dismembered in the world of the spirits of the cycles of time. This must be avoided in a properly ordered esoteric development. Hence those who are able to give instruction for such development see that the necessary precautions are taken that one should not, if possible, allow the 'I' to sleep when the astral body is already awake, for one would then lose inner cohesion and would, like Dionysus, be split up into the whole astral world of the earth, consisting of the spirits of the cycles of time. In a regular esoteric development precautions are taken that this should not occur. These precautions consist in care being taken that the student, who through meditation, concentration or other esoteric exercises is to be stimulated to clairvoyance, should retain two things in the whole sphere of clairvoyant, occult observation. In every esoteric development it is specially important that everything should be so adjusted that two things we possess in ordinary life should not be lost – things we might, however, very easily lose in esoteric development if not rightly guided. If rightly guided, however, we will not lose them. First, we should not lose the recollection of any of the events of our present incarnation, as ordinarily retained in our memory. The connection with memory must not be destroyed. This connection with memory means very much more in the sphere of occultism than it does in the sphere of ordinary life. In ordinary life we understand memory only as the power of looking back and not losing consciousness of the important events of one's life. In occultism, a right memory means that we value with our perceptions and feelings only what we have already accomplished in the past, so that we apply no other value to ourselves or to our deeds than the past deeds themselves deserve. Let us understand this quite correctly, for this is extremely important. If, in the course of one's occult development, one were suddenly driven to say to oneself, 'I am the reincarnation of this or that spirit' – without there being any justification for it through any action of one's own – then one's memory, in an occult sense, would be interrupted. An important principle in occult development is that of attributing no other merit to oneself other than what comes from one's actions in the physical world in the present incarnation. That is extremely important. Any other merit must come only on the basis of a higher development, which can be attained only if one first of all stands firmly on the ground that one esteems oneself for nothing but what one has accomplished in this incarnation. This is quite natural if we look at the matter objectively, for what we have accomplished in the present incarnation is also the result of earlier incarnations; it is that which karma has, so far, made out of us. What karma is still making of us we must first bring about; we must not add that to our value. In short, if we would set a right value on ourselves, we can do so only at the beginning of esoteric development, if we ascribe merit only to what is inscribed in our memory as our past. That is the one element we must preserve, if our 'I' is not to sleep while our astral body is awake.

The second thing that we as people of the present day must not lose is the degree of conscience we possess in the external world. Here again is something that it is extremely important to observe. You must have often experienced that someone you know has gone through an occult development, and if it is not guided and conducted in the right way you find that, in relation to conscience, your friend takes things much more lightly than before the occult training. Before such training, education and social connection were the guides to whether one did this thing or that, or dared not do it. After beginning an occult development, however, many people begin to tell lies who never did so before, and as regards questions of conscience, they take things more lightly. We ought not to lose an iota of the conscience we possess. As regards memory, we must value ourselves only according to what we have already become; not according to any reliance on the future, or on what we are still going to do. As regards conscience, we must retain the same degree of conscience as we acquired in the ordinary physical world. If we retain these two elements in our consciousness, healthy memory that does not deceive us into believing ourselves to be other than our actions prove us to be, and a conscience that does not allow us morally to take things more lightly than before (indeed, if possible, we should take them more seriously!) – if we retain these two qualities, our 'I' will never be asleep when our astral body is awake.

If we can, as it were, remain awake in our sleep and preserve our consciousness and carry it with us into the condition wherein, with our astral body, we are freed from the physical and etheric bodies – if we can do this – then we shall carry the connection with our 'I' into the world in which we awaken with our astral body. Then, if we awake with our 'I', not only do we feel our astral body to be connected with all the spiritual beings we have described as the spirits of the cycles of time of our planet, but we feel in a quite peculiar way that we actually no longer have a direct relation to the individual who is the bearer of the physical and etheric bodies in which we usually live. We feel, so to speak, as if all the qualities of our physical and etheric bodies were taken from us. Then, too, we feel everything taken from us that can only live outwardly in a particular territory of our planet. For what lives on a particular territory of our planet is connected with the spirits of the cycles of time. Now, however, when we waken with our 'I', we feel ourselves not only poured out into the whole world of the spirits of the cycles of time, but we feel ourselves one with the whole undivided spirit of the planet itself; we awaken in the undivided spirit of the planet itself.

It is extremely important that we should feel ourselves as belonging to the whole of our planet. For example, when our occult vision is sufficiently awakened, and we are so far advanced that we can awaken our 'I' and our astral body simultaneously, then our common life with the planet expresses itself in such a way that, just as during our waking hours in the sense world we can follow the sun as it passes over the heavens from morning till night, so now the sun no longer disappears when we fall asleep. When we sleep the sun remains connected with us; it does not cease to shine but takes on a spiritual character, so that while we are actually asleep during the night we can still follow the sun. We human beings are of such a nature that we are connected with the changing conditions of the planet only in so far as we live in the astral body. When, however, we become conscious only of our 'I', we have nothing to do with these changing conditions. But when we awaken our astral body and our 'I' simultaneously then we become conscious of all the conditions which our planet can go through. We then pour ourselves into the whole substance of the planetary spirit.

When I say that we become one with the planetary spirit, that we live in union with this planetary spirit, you must not suppose that this implies an advanced degree of clairvoyance; this is but a beginning. For when we awaken in the manner described we really only experience the planetary spirit as a whole, whereas it consists of many, many differentiations – of wonderful, separate, spiritual beings – as we shall hear in the following lectures. The different parts of the planetary spirit, the special multiplicities of this spirit, of these we are not yet aware. What we realize first of all is the knowledge: 'I live in the planetary spirit as though in a sea, which spiritually bathes the whole planet earth and itself is the spirit of the whole earth.' One may go through immensely long development in order further and further to experience this unification with the planetary spirit; but, to begin with, the experience is as has been described. Just as we say of ourselves as human beings 'behind our astral body is our I', so do we say that behind all that we call the totality of the spirits of the cycles of time is hidden the spirit of the planet itself, the planetary spirit. Whereas the spirits of the cycles of time guide the nature spirits of the elements in order to call forth the rhythmic change and repetitions in time – the alterations in space of the planet earth – the spirit of the earth has a different task. It has the task of bringing the earth itself into mutual relation with the other heavenly bodies in the environment, to direct it and guide it, so that in the course of time it may come into the right relations to the other heavenly bodies. The spirit of the earth is, as it were, the earth's great sense apparatus, through which the planet earth enters into right relationship with the cosmos. If I were to sum up the succession of those spiritual beings with whom we on our earth are first of all concerned, and to whom we can find the way through a gradual occult development, I must say: 'As the first external veil, we have the sense world, with all its multiplicity, with all we see spread out before our senses and which we can understand with our human mind; then, behind this sense world, we have the world of nature spirits. Behind this world of nature spirits we have the spirits of the cycles of time, and behind these the planetary spirit'.

If you wish to compare what normal consciousness knows about the structure of the cosmos with the structure of the cosmos itself, you may make that clear in the following way. We will take it that the most external veil is this world of the senses, behind which is the world of the nature spirits, and behind that the spirits of the cycles of time and behind that the planetary spirit. Now, we must say that the planetary spirit in its activity in a certain respect penetrates through to the sense world, so that in a certain way we can perceive its image in the sense world. This also applies to the spirits of the cycles of time, as well as to the nature spirits. So, if we observe the sense world itself with normal consciousness, we can see in the background, as it were, the impression, the traces, of those worlds that lie behind – as if we drew aside the sense world as the outermost skin, and behind this we had different degrees of active spiritual beings. Normal consciousness realizes the sense world by means of its perceptions; the world of nature spirits expresses itself from behind these perceptions as what we call the forces of nature. When science speaks of the forces of nature, we have there nothing that is actually real; to the occultist the forces of nature are not realities but *maya*, imprints of the nature spirits working behind the world of sense.

Again, the imprint of the spirits of the cycles of time is what is usually known to ordinary consciousness as the laws of nature. Fundamentally, all the laws of nature are in existence because the spirits of the cycles of time work as the directing powers. To the occultist, the laws of nature are not realities. Whereas the ordinary natural scientist speaks of the laws of nature and combines them externally, the occultist knows that these laws are revealed in their reality when, in his awakened astral body, he listens to what the spirits of the cycles of time say, and hears how they order and direct the nature spirits. That is expressed in *maya* – in external semblance – as the laws of nature, and normal consciousness, as a rule, does not go beyond this. It does not usually reach the imprint of the planetary spirit in the external world. The normal consciousness of contemporary humanity speaks of the external world of perception, of the facts that can be perceived. It speaks of the forces of nature, light, warmth, magnetism, electricity, and so on; of the forces of attraction and repulsion, of gravity, and so forth. These are the beings of *maya*, semblance, behind which, in reality, lies the world of nature spirits – the etheric body of the earth. External science also speaks of the laws of nature, but that again is *maya*. Underlying these laws is what we have described as the world of the spirits of the cycles of time. Only when we penetrate still

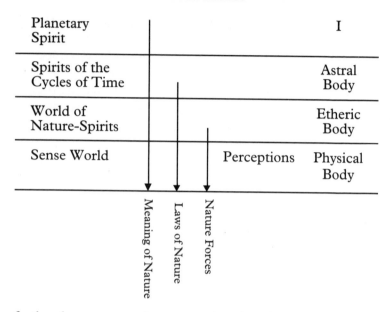

Planetary Spirit				I
Spirits of the Cycles of Time				Astral Body
World of Nature-Spirits				Etheric Body
Sense World			Perceptions	Physical Body

Meaning of Nature   Laws of Nature   Nature Forces

further do we come to the stamp or imprint of the planetary spirit itself in the external sense world. Science today does not do this. Those who still do so are no longer quite believed. The poets, the artists do – they seek for a meaning behind things. Why does the plant world blossom? Why do the different species of animals arise and disappear? Why do human beings inhabit the earth? If we thus enquire into the phenomena of nature and wish to analyse their meaning and to combine the external facts as even a deeper philosophy still sometimes tries to do, we then approach the imprint of the planetary spirit itself in the external world. Today, however, nobody really believes any longer in this seeking after the meaning of existence. Through feeling, one still believes a little, but science no longer wishes to know what could be discovered about the laws of nature by studying the passage of the phenomena.

If we still seek a meaning as to the laws of nature in the things of the world perceptible to our senses, we should be able to interpret this meaning as the imprint of the planetary spirit in the sense world. That would be the external *maya*. In the first place, the sense world itself is an external *maya* or semblance, for it is what the etheric body of the earth, the substance of the nature spirits, drives out of itself. A second *maya* is what appears to us of the nature spirits in the forces of nature A third *maya* is what appears as the laws of nature, coming from the spirits of the cycles of time. A fourth maya is something that, in spite of its *maya* nature, speaks to the human soul because, in the perception of the purpose of nature, we at any rate feel ourselves united with the spirit of the whole planet, with the spirit that leads the planet through cosmic space and gives meaning, in fact, to the whole planet. In this *maya* lies the direct imprint of the planetary spirit itself.

Thus we may say that we have today ascended to the undivided spirit of the planet. If again we wish to compare what we have now discovered about the planet with the human being, we may say: 'The sense world corresponds to the human physical body, the world of nature spirits to the human etheric body, the world of the spirits of the cycles of time to the human astral body, and the planetary spirit to the human "I".' Just as the human 'I' perceives the physical environment of earth, so does the planetary spirit perceive everything in the periphery and in cosmic space as a whole outside the planet; it adjusts the acts of the planet and also the feelings of the planet, according to these perceptions of cosmic space. For what a planet does outside in space, when it passes on its way in cosmic distances, and what it effects in its own body, in the elements of which it consists, that again is the result of the observations of the planetary spirit with regard to the external world. Just as the individual human soul lives in the world of the earth side by side with other human beings and adjusts to them, so does the planetary spirit live in its planetary body, which is the ground on which we stand. But this planetary spirit lives in fellowship with other planetary spirits, other spirits of the heavenly bodies.

III. Redemption of the Elementals by the Human Being

Dusseldorf, 12 April 1909

THE TEACHINGS proclaimed by the Holy Rishis during the first post-Atlantean period arose from purely spiritual sources.[20] The important characteristic of this teaching or mode of investigation is that it penetrated deeply into natural processes and discovered the active, spiritual principles underlying them. Fundamentally speaking, we are continually surrounded by spiritual happenings and beings. Physical phenomena are merely the expression of spiritual deeds, and things that appear to us in material form are the outward sheaths of spiritual beings. Now, when the primeval divine teaching spoke of perceptible phenomena in our surroundings, particular emphasis was laid on what, to them, was the most important natural phenomenon surrounding man on earth – fire. In all explanations of what occurred upon the earth a central position was allotted to the spiritual investigation of fire. If we seek to understand oriental teachings about fire, so important in ancient times for all knowledge and life, we shall have to consider how other natural phenomena were regarded in the past by a teaching still valid in the spiritual science of today.

In these ancient times, all that surrounded people materially in the world was referred back to the four elements. The four elements, earth, water, air and fire, are no longer acknowledged by modern materialistic science. But with the word 'earth' the spiritual science of that time did not mean what is meant by the word today. 'Earth' denoted a condition of matter, the solid state. In spiritual science everything to which we refer as solid was called 'earthy'. No matter whether it was a solid lump of arable soil, a crystal, a piece of lead or gold, or anything of a solid nature, it was termed 'earth'. Everything fluid, not only water as we know it, was referred to as 'watery' or 'water'. If you take iron, for example, and melt it by means of fire so that it becomes fluid, spiritual science would refer to it in that condition as 'water'. All metals in the fluid state were termed 'water'. What we call gaseous was termed 'air', irrespective of the particular gas to which it applied, whether oxygen, hydrogen or some other gas.

Fire was the fourth element. Those of you who are familiar with elementary physics will remember that modern science does not regard fire as comparable with earth, water or air. Fire, according to modern physics, is merely looked upon as a condition of movement. For spiritual science, however, warmth or fire is something endowed with an even finer substantiality than air. Just as 'earth', or solidity, can be transformed into the liquid state, so, according to spiritual science, all 'airy' or gaseous forms gradually change into the condition of 'fire'. Fire is so rarefied that it permeates all other elements. It permeates 'air' and thereby warms it; the same applies to 'water' and 'earth'. Whereas the three other elements are separate, the element 'fire' possesses an all-pervading quality.

Now, both ancient and modern spiritual science agree that there is a still more important difference between what we term earth, water, air and what we call fire or warmth. How do we get to know the earth element or solidity? We might try by touching it and experiencing its resistance. The same applies to water though it offers less resistance. Nevertheless we are aware of it as something external to ourselves, as a resistance. The same is true of air. We only get to know it externally in relation to ourselves. But this is not the case with warmth. Here we shall have to emphasize an aspect that is regarded as unimportant by the modern outlook, but we shall have to consider it if we wish to fathom the riddles of existence. We do, in fact, become aware of warmth without touching it externally. That is the important point. We become aware of warmth by touching an object that has been heated, in which case we become aware of it in the same way as we do the other elements, but we also feel the warmth within our own organism. That is why the ancient knowledge of the Hindus stressed that we only become aware of earth, water and air in the outer world. Warmth is the first element that can also be apprehended inwardly. Warmth, or fire, has a twofold nature – an external aspect, which we get to know outwardly, and an inner aspect, which we feel in our own condition of warmth. Actually, we feel our own inner warmth, we are hot or cold, and yet one is little inclined to concern oneself with what is gaseous, watery or solid in one's organism, that is, with what is air, water and earth in ourselves. We only begin to be aware of ourselves in the element of warmth. Ancient and modern spiritual science both proclaim fire or warmth to be the first stage at which matter becomes soul. Hence, we can speak in the full sense of the word of an outer fire, which we perceive as we do other elements, and of an inner soul fire within man.

That is why, in spiritual science, fire always built a bridge between the outer material world, and the inner soul world that can be perceived only inwardly. Fire or warmth was central to all observation of nature; it was the gateway by means of which one penetrated from the outer to the inner. It is truly like a door in front of which one can stand. One can behold it from outside, one can open it, and one can behold it from within. That is the true place of fire among natural phenomena.

Let us now consider an elementary lesson in primal human wisdom. The teacher in the past would ask that an object being consumed by fire be observed and would then point out that two things were to be seen. In olden times one was called 'smoke' (the term still applies today) and the other was called 'light'. The spiritual scientist saw fire as placed between light and smoke, and the teacher would say that both are born out of the flame.

Now, we should bear in mind a simple, yet most important, characteristic with regard to the light that is born of the fire. Most people, if you were to ask them if they see light, would reply that they do, of course. Yet this is absolutely erroneous because the physical eye cannot, in fact, perceive the light. We see objects, be they solid, fluid or gaseous, because of the light, but the light itself we cannot see. Imagine the whole of universal space illumined by a light, the source of which was behind you where you could not see it. Then imagine you were to look into the world-spaces illuminated through and through by that light. Would you see the light? You would see absolutely nothing. You would only perceive something when an object was placed within the illuminated space. One cannot see light but only the solid, fluid and gaseous elements through the effects of the light. Spiritual science, therefore, says that light makes everything visible but cannot itself be seen. This is an important statement; light is imperceptible. It cannot be perceived by means of our external senses. We can perceive the solid, the fluid and the gaseous, and we can still perceive outwardly warmth or fire, but here an inner perception begins. The light as such can no longer be perceived externally. If you think that when you look at the sun you see the light, then you are quite mistaken. You see a burning body, a burning substance that emanates light. You can prove it to yourself. You do not see the light but only the burning object.

So, according to spiritual science, we rise upward from earth to water, from air to fire and then to light. That is to say, we pass from the outward-perceptible to the invisible, the spiritual etheric realm. Or one might say, fire is situated at the boundary between the perceptible, material world and the etheric, spiritual realm that is no longer perceptible. What happens to an object consumed by fire? Light is produced. In fact, heat, if it is sufficiently intense, produces a source of light that is outwardly imperceptible, but which reaches upwards into the spiritual worlds. A part is given over to the invisible world but it must pay for this in the form of smoke. Out of the part that was first transparent and translucent, an opaque 'smoky' portion is separated off. So we see how fire or warmth is divided into two components. It divides itself off towards the light, thus opening up a path toward the supersensible, but as a result it also has to send something down into the opaque, perceptible, material world. Every form of existence has two aspects. Thus, where we have light as a result of heat we also find opaque, dark matter appearing. That is an ancient, basic teaching of spiritual science.

That, however, is only the outer physical aspect of the process. At its foundation lies something still essentially different. When an object is heated but does not produce any light, the generated warmth that one can perceive with the senses also contains a spiritual element. When the heat becomes so intense that light arises and smoke is produced, a part of the spiritual component that was in the heat goes over into smoke. The spiritual component of warmth, which was in the fire and which was then transformed in a gaseous element, is bewitched in the opaque smoke. Spiritual beings connected with fire have, so to speak, to allow themselves to be made opaque, to be bewitched in the smoke. Thus, everything of a turbid nature, of the solidification connected with warmth, is associated with the bewitchment of spiritual beings.

We can put it even more simply. Let us imagine that air is made liquid, a process that can be achieved today. Now, air is mere solidified warmth, densified warmth as a result of the smoke that has been formed. The spiritual part that should by rights be in the fire has been bewitched into the smoke. Spiritual beings, which may also be called elemental beings, are bewitched in the air and are still more deeply bewitched in a yet lower form of existence when air is transformed into the liquid state. That is why spiritual science sees in all physically perceptible things an element that has proceeded out of an original condition of fire or warmth. It became air, smoke or gaseous as the warmth densified into gas, the gas became liquid, and the liquid densified into the solid state. 'Look backwards,' says the spiritual scientist. 'Look at any solid substance. Once it was fluid. It has only become solid in the course of evolution. The liquid was once gaseous and the gaseous state arose out of the smoke that proceeded from the fire. But a bewitchment of spiritual beings is connected with each stage of densification.'

Now let us look at the world that surrounds us. The solid stones, the streams, the evaporating water that rises as mist, the air – all things that are solid, liquid or gaseous – are, in fact, densified fire. Gold, silver and copper are densified fire. In the far distant past everything was fire; everything was born of fire, but in all forms of densification spiritual beings lie bewitched!

How are the spiritual divine beings that surround us able to produce solid matter as it exists on our planet? How do they produce liquid and airy substances? They send down elemental beings that dwell in fire, and imprison them in the air, water and earth. They are emissaries, elemental messengers of the spiritual, creative, formative beings. At first, elemental beings live in the fire and, to put it pictorially, they feel comfortable there. Then they are condemned to an existence of bewitchment. We can say as we look around us, 'The beings whom we have to thank for everything that surrounds us had to descend from the fire element and are bewitched in the things of this world.'

Are human beings able to help these elemental beings in some way or other? That is the great question that was put by the Holy Rishis. Are we able to release them? Yes, we can. For the deeds of man on earth are nothing but the external expression of spiritual processes. Everything we do here is also of importance for the spiritual world. Let us consider the following. A person stands in front of a crystal, a lump of gold or the like. He looks at it. What happens if a person simply stares, simply looks at some object by means of his physical senses? A continual interplay arises between man and the bewitched elemental being. That which is bewitched in matter and man are in some way related to one another. Let us assume, however, that he merely stares at the object so that he only takes in what is impressed upon his eye. Something is continually passing from these elementals into man, and it goes on from morning until night. As we look out into the world, hosts of elementals, who were or who are continually being bewitched into the processes of densification, are continually entering into us from our surroundings.

Now let us assume that such a person, as he stares at an object, has not the slightest inclination to reflect about what he sees, or to let the spirit of things live in his soul. He takes the easy road; he goes through the world but does not digest his experiences spiritually by means of thoughts and feelings. He remains a mere spectator of the physical, material world. In that case, the elemental beings enter into him and remain there. They have gained nothing in the world process and have merely transferred their seat from the outer world into that of man. But now let us take a person who digests his impressions spiritually by thinking about them, and by form-ing concepts about the underlying spiritual foundation of the world. That is, a person who does not merely stare but ponders over its nature, a person who feels the beauty of things and ennobles his impressions. What does such a person do? As a result of his spiritual activity he redeems the elemental being that streams towards him from the outer world, thus raising it to its previous state. He releases the elemental being from its enchantment. So, through our spiritual activity, we can release beings who are bewitched in air, water and earth and lead them back to their former condition, or we can imprison them again in our inner being without any transformation having taken place in them. Throughout the whole of man's life on earth, elemental beings stream into him. It depends on him whether they remain unchanged or whether he releases them.

What happens to the elemental beings who have been

released by man's activity? To begin with, they too inhabit man. Even those who have been released dwell in man until he dies. When a person goes through the gate of death, there is a distinction between these elemental beings who merely entered into him and have not been led back to the higher elements and those who, through man's activity, have been guided back to their former condition. Those who have not been transformed have gained nothing by wandering from the outer world into man; others are able to return to their former condition after man's death. During life on earth man builds a crossroad for elementals. When man has gone through life in the spiritual worlds and returns in a subsequent incarnation through the gate of birth, all elemental beings whom he did not release, accompany him into physical existence. Those whom he releases do not accompany him any longer; they return to their original condition.

What happens when a person looks at a material object and fathoms its true nature so that the elemental being is thereby released? Spiritually, the reverse course is taken from what occurred formerly. Whereas originally smoke arose out of the fire, man now spiritually creates fire out of smoke. The fire, however, is only released at his death. We can now understand the profound spiritual meaning of ancient rituals of sacrifice when considered in the light of the primeval, divine spiritual science. Imagine the priest at the sacrificial altar in those ancient times when religion rested upon a true knowledge of spiritual laws. Imagine the priest kindling the flame, and the rising smoke, the object of sacrifice, as it is accompanied upwards by prayers. What really happened in such sacrifices? The priest stood at the altar where the smoke was produced. There, where the solid emerged out of the warmth, a spirit was bewitched, but as a man accompanied the process with prayers, the spirit went over into him and was released into the supersensible world after his death. What did the priest of the ancient Mysteries say to those who learned to understand such a ritual? He explained that if you look at the external world in such a way that your spiritual activity does not remain attached to the smoke, but rises spiritually to the fire element, then, after death, you free the bewitched spirit that dwells in the smoke. The human being who had gained an understanding of the process would reply, 'If the spirit that dwells in the smoke remains unchanged, it will have to accompany me in a next incarnation; after death it will be unable to return to the spiritual world. If I have released it, if I have led it back to the fire, after my death it will arise into worlds of spirit and no longer need to return to earth at my birth.'

Here we have explained a part of the profound passage from the *Bhagavad Gita* of which I spoke in my last lecture. There is no mention of the human ego. It refers, rather, to nature beings, to elemental beings that enter into man from the outer world saying, 'Behold the fire, behold the smoke; what man turns into fire through his spiritual activity are spirits that he liberates at his death.' What he leaves untransformed in the smoke remains connected with him after death and has to be born when he is born again. The destiny of elemental spirits is here described. Through his wisdom man continually liberates elemental beings at his death; through his lack of wisdom, through a materialistic attachment to the world of the senses, he ties elemental spirits to him and forces them into this world to be reborn ever and again with him.

These elemental beings, however, are not only connected with fire. They are emissaries of higher divine spiritual beings and are involved in everything that takes place in the external perceptible world. The inter-play of day and night, for example, could not have arisen unless hosts of elemental beings had been active rotating the planets in the universe in the appropriate manner. Everything that happens is determined by hosts of lower and higher beings of the Spiritual Hierarchies. We have been speaking of the lowest order, of the messengers. Elemental beings live in the processes that transform night into day and day into night, and man is again closely connected with beings of the elemental world whose function it is to bring about day and night. A person who is apathetic and lazy, and lets himself go, affects these elemental beings quite differently from one who is creative, active, diligent and productive. When a person is lazy, for instance, he unites himself with certain kinds of elemental beings and this also happens when he is active, but in another way. The elemental beings of the second class to whom we have referred are active during the day and are then in an ascending phase. But just as fire-elementals of the first class are bound to air, water and earth, so are certain elementals bound to darkness. Day could not be separated from night unless elementals were imprisoned into night. Man is able to enjoy daylight thanks to divine spiritual beings who have driven forth elementals and have chained them to night. When a person is lazy, these elementals continually flow into him unchanged. Through his idleness he leaves unchanged those elemental beings who are chained to darkness at night. Those elemental beings who enter into him when he is active and industrious are led back into the daylight. Thus, he continually releases elementals of the second class. Throughout the whole of our lives we carry elemental beings in us who have either entered during periods of idleness or industry. As we go through the gate of death, those beings whom we have led back to the day can enter the spiritual world. Beings whom we have left in the night as a result of our apathy remain chained to us and return with us at our next incarnation. This brings us to the second point in the passage of the *Bhagavad Gita*. Again it is not the human ego that is being referred to in the following words but the type of elemental beings: 'Behold day and night. What you redeem, what you transform from a being of night into a being of day, enters into higher worlds when you die. What you take with you as a being of the night you condemn to accompany you in a succeeding incarnation.'

Now you will no doubt guess how the matter proceeds. The same holds true of more encompassing natural phenomena such as the twenty-eight-day rhythm that brings about the waxing and waning moon. Hosts of elemental beings had to be active to bring the moon into movement so that the moon-rhythm and everything connected with it might arise visible for us on earth. This again meant that certain of these elementals had to be bewitched, condemned and imprisoned by higher beings. Supersensible cognition always notices that during the time of a waxing moon spiritual beings of a lower realm rise into a higher. But so that order might prevail, other spiritual elemental beings have to be bewitched as a result into lower realms.

These elementals of the third kind are also connected with man. A person who is bright and cheerful, who is satisfied with life, who is of a cheerful disposition because of his understanding of the world, is continually liberating beings who are chained because of the waning moon. These beings enter into him but are continually released because of his serene soul disposition, his inner contentment, his harmonious view of life. Beings who enter into man when he is sullen, peevish, discontented with everything, depressed and pessimistic remain in the condition of bewitchment in which they were at the time of the waning moon. There are human beings who, through the fact that they have achieved a harmonious feeling about the world and a cheerful disposition, work in a wonderfully liberating way on large numbers of elementals. Thus we see that man's mood is not only of significance for himself, but a cheerful or a morose attitude can bring about either forces of liberation or of imprisonment. The effects of a person's moods stream out in all directions into the spiritual world. Here we have the third point in the important teaching of the *Bhagavad Gita*: 'Behold the man who, through his mood of soul, releases during the time of the waxing moon spirits that return to higher worlds at his death.'

Finally, we have a fourth kind of elemental being. These

activate the course of the sun during the year and bring about the wakening, fruitful activity of the sun during the summer so that the ripening that takes place from spring to autumn may come about. As a result, certain spirits have to be chained, bewitched, during the winter period. Here, too, man works as has been described for the other degrees of spiritual beings of the elemental realms. Let us take a person who says to himself at the approach of winter, 'The nights are becoming longer, the days shorter. We are approaching a time of year when the sun withdraws its ripening forces from the earth. Outwardly, the earth is dying but as this process takes place, I feel all the more the need to awaken spiritually. I must receive the spirit into myself evermore.'

Let us take a person who, with the approach of Christmas, carries an ever greater feeling of devotion in his heart, one who understands the true meaning of this festival, which is that as outer nature dies the spirit must be all the more awake. Let us assume such a person lives through the winter season and at Easter realizes that the time of sleep for the spirit is connected with the enlivening processes in nature. He then experiences the Easter festival with understanding. Such a person does not merely possess an external religiosity but a religious understanding of the processes in nature, for the spirit that dwells in nature. By means of this kind of devotion he is able to liberate elementals of the fourth class that continually stream in and out of man and are connected with the course of the sun. A person not endowed with this kind of devotion, one who denies the spirit and who is caught up by our materialistic chaos, is entered by elementals of the fourth class who stream into him and remain as they are. At man's death these elementals are either released, or chained so that they must reappear in the world at his rebirth. He who connects himself to the winter spirits without transforming them into summer spirits, that is, without redeeming them through his spiritual activity, condemns them to be reborn with him. If the opposite is the case, they will not have to return with him.

Behold the fire and the smoke! If you so connect yourself with the outer world that your soul-spiritual activity is akin to the process that brings about fire and smoke, if you spiritualize the things around you through your knowledge and your feelings, then you assist spiritual elemental beings to ascend again. If you connect yourself with the smoke, you condemn them to rebirth. If you connect yourself with the day, you again liberate certain spirits. Behold the light, behold the day, the waxing moon, the summer season of the year! If you are active in such a way that elementals are led back to the light, the day, the waxing moon and the summer season of the year, you free those elemental beings whom you need so very much; at your death they rise into the spiritual world. If you connect yourself with the smoke, staring at solid matter, or if you connect yourself to the night through apathy, to the spirits of the waning moon because of your ill-humour, and to the spirits who are chained in the winter time through godlessness or lack of spirituality, then you condemn elemental beings to reincarnate with you.

Now we begin to understand what is really meant by this passage of the *Bhagavad Gita*. The one who thinks it refers to human beings does not understand it. He who knows, however, that all human life is a continual interplay between man and the spiritual beings that live around him, that these four groups of elemental beings are bewitched and need to be liberated, recognizes their ascension or their need to reincarnate. The mystery regarding the lowest rung of hierarchical beings has been preserved for us in this passage of the *Bhagavad Gita*. When one has to draw forth from primeval wisdom what is proclaimed in ancient religious documents, one begins to realize their true greatness and how wrong it is to take them superficially, thereby avoiding plumbing their depths. One only gains a right relation to them when one says that no wisdom is exalted enough to fathom what is contained in them. Then the ancient records become permeated by the magic of devoted feelings, and only then do they become what they truly are: ennobling and purifying means for human evolution. Still, they point to fathomless abysses of human wisdom. Only when that which springs from the occult schools and Mysteries begins to stream from man outwards to humanity at large, only then will the reflections of primeval wisdom (and they are but reflections) be seen in their true greatness.

We have attempted to show by means of a comparatively difficult example the knowledge that existed in primeval wisdom of the interplay between man and the beings that surround him and stream in and out of him, of the interplay that arises between the spiritual world and man's inner world as a result of his deeds. The riddle of man becomes important for us when we begin to realize that in all we do, even down to our moods, we influence the whole cosmos, that our little world is of infinitely far-reaching importance for all that comes into being in the macrocosmos. A heightened feeling of responsibility is the finest and most important fruit that can be gained from spiritual science. It teaches us to grasp the true sense of life, to take it earnestly so that what we cast upon the stream of evolution may be meaningful.

IV. Gnomes, Undines, Sylphs and Salamanders

Berlin, 16 May 1908

WE SHALL today make the acquaintance of beings who may be said to be among us, if we regard ourselves as spiritual beings, but to whom we have so far paid little attention in our studies. We have, as you know, always set man in the centre of our world conception, as the microcosm. To understand man and his evolution, however, we have been giving most attention to other beings, to higher spiritual beings who formerly played that part in our earth evolution which is played today by man. We have seen that before our earth entered on its present stage, it was what we have become accustomed to call the Old Moon. And we know that certain spiritual beings who today stand higher than man were then passing through their human stage, although under different conditions.

We have learnt that beings who are today two stages higher than man, the Fire Spirits, went through their human stage on the Old Sun, and we have further learnt that the Asuras went through the human stage on Old Saturn. Their qualities, good as well as evil, stand far above or below those of man. Thus in the course of time we have reviewed a whole series of beings who participate in the whole development of our life and nature. We have come to know beings to whom in a certain respect we must look up; and one who can observe clairvoyantly finds a significant distinction between them and man. You know that we differentiate various members of man's nature. We apportion to him a bodily nature – the physical body, etheric body, astral body – and, distinct from the body, a soul-nature – sentient soul, intellectual soul, consciousness soul – and thirdly, a spirit which is only in the initial stages of evolution. In the future phases of our planet man will bring it to a higher development.

When we examine the human being we therefore find him consisting of three parts, a bodily, a soul, and a spiritual part, which broadly speaking make up the threefold being of man. If we now look up from man to the higher beings of whom we have just spoken, we may say that they differ from man by not having developed the coarse body. Those beings, for instance, whom we call Lunar Pitris, or angels in Christian esotericism, possess no coarse bodily nature perceptible to the senses. They passed through the stage of humanity on the Old Moon and have now ascended higher. Such a coarse corporeal nature as man's cannot be attributed to them. On the other hand they have already developed the higher members of the spirit not yet possessed by man, so that we can say that they are spirit and soul, in contrast to man, who is a three-membered being – spirit, soul, body.

Thus, we have been occupying ourselves principally with cosmic beings who stand above man and have spirit and soul. For the occult observer, however, still other beings exist in the world, and although in the modern phase of human development they are largely concealed they nevertheless play a part in evolution. There are beings which clairvoyant sight cannot recognize as spiritual, for what we are accustomed to call spirit in man cannot be discovered in them: they consist essentially of body and soul.

Now from our previous studies you know a whole group of such beings, that is, the animals. They have body and soul. We know, however, that the animals are connected with their so-called group ego, and that this is itself of a spiritual nature. In the single animal standing before us in the physical world we have indeed a being possessing only body and soul, but it is continued, as it were, towards the higher worlds and linked to spirituality. I have often used a certain comparison in respect of the animal group ego: if there were a partition here and I stretched my fingers through it without your seeing me, but only the ten fingers, you would yet say that the fingers must come from someone who is invisible to you. It is just the same with the group egos; they are invisible and concealed for physical perception, but they exist nevertheless. The animal belongs to a group and the various animal groups are connected with the group egos above. It is therefore only when we refer to the single animal here on the physical plane that we can say animals have body and soul. What we see has a continuation into the astral.

But other beings exist which are no longer visible to the physical senses, beings possessing body and soul. In various occult teachings they are often called elemental spirits. To call them elemental spirits shows the greatest possible ineptitude, for it is just spirit that they do not possess. It is better to call them elemental beings, and we shall see shortly why their bodies are not visible. In the meantime let us accept as a kind of definition that such beings consist of body and soul. Their existence is of course denied in our enlightened age, for man in his present phase of development cannot see them; one who wishes to see them must have progressed to a certain degree of clairvoyant consciousness. The fact that a thing is not perceptible does not mean, however, that it is not active in our world. The activity of these beings of body and soul plays very definitely into our world. What they do can very well be seen, but not the doers themselves.

Now our first concern is to gain as far as is possible without definite perception some idea of these elemental beings which take various forms and occupy the spiritual realm that has received us all. They are also spoken of as 'nature spirits'; in fact, they have been given many different names. The name, however, does not matter; what is necessary is that we create a certain concept of them. And here already comes an appeal to your advanced feelings and perceptions. I should like to relate quite simply and plainly how such beings show themselves to clairvoyant sight.

There are beings that can be seen with clairvoyant vision at many spots in the depths of the earth, especially places little touched by living growths, places, for instance, in a mine which have always been of a mineral nature. If you dig into metallic or stony ground you find beings which manifest at first in remarkable fashion – it is as if something were to scatter us. They seem able to crouch close together in vast numbers, and when the earth is laid open they appear to burst asunder. The important point is that they do not fly apart into a certain number but that in their own bodily nature they become larger. Even when they reach their greatest size, they are still always small creatures in comparison with human beings. The enlightened man knows nothing of them. People, however, who have preserved a certain nature-sense, i.e. the old clairvoyant forces which everyone once possessed and which had to be lost with the acquisition of objective consciousness, could tell you all sorts of things about such beings. Many names have been given to them, such as goblins, gnomes, and so forth. Apart from the fact that their body is invisible, they differ essentially from man inasmuch as one could never reasonably attribute to them any kind of moral responsibility. What one calls moral responsibility in man is entirely lacking in them; what they do, they do automatically, and at the same time it is not at all unlike what the human intellect, intelligence, does. They possess what one calls wit in the highest degree and anyone coming into touch with them can observe good proofs of this. Their nature prompts them to play all sorts of tricks on man, as every miner can tell you who has still preserved something of a healthy nature-sense – not so much the miners in coal mines as those in metal mines.

The different members of these beings can be investigated by occult means just as in the case of man when we distinguish his members as physical body, etheric body, astral body, and ego, and what is to evolve from them as Spirit-Self, Life-Spirit and Spirit-Man. In his present phase of development man consists essentially of the four members first named, so that we can say that his highest member is the ego or 'I' and the lowest is the physical body.

But now we should succumb to delusion if we imagined quite

abstractly that the physical body had nothing to do with man's ego. In man's physical body we have the instrument for the human ego. We have seen that the human body is a very complicated organization. In all essentials the ego has its physical instrument in the blood, the astral body in the nervous system, the etheric body in the glandular system, the physical body in the physical organs working purely mechanically. We must picture to ourselves that all the human inner experience that goes on in the astral body has its material expression in the nervous system, and all that goes on in the etheric body finds its material expression in the glandular system, the instrument of the etheric body. Thus the physical body presents, as it were, an image of the fourfold being of man.

Now take the human physical body as you have it before you, take all that this physical body is as instrument of the thinking ego. You will best realize what is meant by this when you remember that the ego itself remains the same from incarnation to incarnation, but that the instrument of the ego is built up anew for each incarnation. The material tool of the ego is built up anew in each incarnation. Now man has an advantage over the whole animal kingdom in possessing a finer material organization, namely, the material organization that manifests the actual human intelligence. And this has come into existence through the fact that for long periods of time the ego has slowly and gradually learnt – although unconsciously – to work upon the astral body.

We know that man's astral body consists of two parts – one part upon which he has as yet done nothing, which is therefore as it was macrocosmically, and one part upon which he has worked. These two parts are in a certain way developed in everyone. In the higher nervous system, particularly in the brain which is built afresh with each new incarnation, you have the material expression of the work done by man's ego upon his astral body. Thus man has a much more completely developed forebrain than the animal because the front part of the brain is the manifestation of the astral body worked upon by the ego. But the astral body has nevertheless its outer expression in the nervous system as well.

Now you can easily realize that the moment some member of our organism is brought to a higher stage of perfection, an alteration must take place in the whole remaining organism. The rest of the organism must undergo a change. Why cannot a person go on four feet? Why has he transformed his front limbs into instruments of work? Because in his earthly development he has worked upon his astral body! To develop the forebrain involves perfecting the etheric instrument. The outer is always a real manifestation of the inner. All that we see in a physical state in our present phase of evolution is a result, and indeed a specific result, of spiritual evolution.

Now you will realize that everything material, right into the form, is a result of what stands actively behind this material. There are, for instance, beings like those I have just described to you which are unable to transform their astral body because they lack a spiritual nature. No ego works upon their astral body. This astral body with all its soul-experiences must come to expression in a material form. Yet the material form of beings through which no ego glows cannot be visible in our evolutionary phase. It cannot be visible because it lies one degree lower than our visible matter. I beg you to grasp clearly what is meant by that. If one tries to describe what constitutes a physical body, one can say that one sees it. One cannot see the etheric body because as regards substance it lies a stage higher than the physical body. Still less can one see the astral body because it lies higher still. But beneath physical matter there are also substances which cannot be seen. Of all matter only a middle strip or band is perceptible, just that strip which constitutes physical matter, perceptible to the physical eye. Just as substance continues upwards as physical foundation for the etheric and astral, so does it continue downwards and again becomes invisible. And now that we have considered the different members of the human being we shall be able to set before us the membering of these other beings.

What we call elemental beings lack an ego, but they have developed a principle below the physical body. We can say, therefore, that the principles 3, 2, 1 and minus 1 are developed in them. But there are not only beings which begin at the third principle. We have also those which begin at 2 and then have minus 1 and minus 2. And then we have still others whose highest principle is the same as man's lowest. They have developed 1, minus 1, minus 2 and minus 3. If they have a physical body it must be an invisible one. We can also say that if man's higher members were not there his physical body would look very different. When he dies the physical body is alone and disintegrates into the atoms of nature. That it is as we know it today is because it is interpenetrated by etheric body, astral body and ego. It is true that the beings which we call gnomes and goblins have a physical body, but they do not possess what in man we call the ego. The gnomes have the physical body as their highest principle, but they have three principles below the physical body. That makes their bodies far less visible than the physical body of man. The forces lying below the physical plane prevent even what is physical in them from ever being visible to the ordinary eye. If they are to have something approaching physical substance, it can only come about under powerful pressure, if external physical matter presses them together. Then their corporeality is so compressed that they lie in a congested mass and develop in the gruesome way I described earlier. The process when the outer pressure is removed, when the earth is dug away, is in general one of dissolving which is accomplished with immense rapidity, far quicker than the dissolution of the human body after death. Hence they can never be seen even though they have a physical body. They have a physical body only for one who can see through the earth. As far as the principle, the force, of this body is concerned there is something in its structure and organization which resembles the human instrument of thought. Hence those persons who portray gnomes out of a certain nature-sense are not unjustified in making their heads a special characteristic. All these symbols have their true foundation in reality. These beings have a sort of automatic intelligence because it really acts automatically. It is as if you imagine your brain to be taken out. It will not then be interpenetrated by your higher members, and as soon as it is taken out it no longer acts with higher intelligence. In this way we have before us the beings that we call gnomes. We shall then be able to throw further light on the beings that stand below man. But first we must form an idea as to where such beings stand in the course of evolution. This question is in fact by far the more important one, and is connected not only with our past evolution, but also with that in the future. That is the essential thing. And how are they connected with our future evolution?

To answer this we must consider the development of man. We know that man passes from embodiment to embodiment, from incarnation to incarnation; we know that to each new incarnation he brings with him the fruits of the previous one. We know that in each new incarnation man himself is actually a co-creator of his form as well as of his abilities and destiny. What meets him as his destiny are the deeds which he himself formerly engraved into the external world. They come back again as his destiny. What he has engraved into himself through his life comes back to him as his talents and faculties. Thus man shares in creating both – his external destiny and his inner organization.

We now ask ourselves: 'Where does this come from? What is it that causes us to be, let us say, at a more perfect stage of development (and every single person is at a more perfect stage in this respect)? What makes us advance to a higher stage?' It is all that we have taken in throughout our incarnations. We do not see through our eyes and hear through our ears to no purpose; after death we assimilate the fruits of a life and bring with us what can be effective, that from which we can build the germinal force of the next incarnation.

Now various things can occur. The little pointer of the balance can swing out towards the one or the other side. The ideal condition would be that a person in each incarnation made a thorough use of his life, that he left unused nothing which he could go through and experience and which could bear fruit for the following incarnation, but that he took everything with him. This as a rule never happens. A person oversteps either to the one side or to the other. He either uses his organization insufficiently, certain forces remain unused and he brings less into the new incarnation than he could have done, or he penetrates too deeply into his organization and becomes too closely involved in his bodily nature. There are two sorts of people. The one kind would like to live entirely in the spirit and not descend to their corporeal nature; they are called dreamers and visionaries by ordinary everyday people. The other kind descend too deeply into the body. They do not draw out from the incarnation what should be drawn out, but grow together with the incarnation. They find it sympathetic and pleasant to be with the incarnation; they do not keep for themselves what progresses from incarnation to incarnation but let it sink down into what ought only to be the instrument for the eternal germ of man's being.

I pointed once before to an important legend that sets before us what a person must experience who descends too deeply into the temporary, transitory nature of the one incarnation. If we think of an extreme case, we can imagine it like this: 'What is it to me that I should carry over something to later incarnations? I live in this incarnation, I like it, it suits me very well. I am not concerned further with what I am supposed to make from it.' If this thought is followed up, where does it lead? It leads to a person who sits at the wayside when a great Leader of humanity passes by. He, however, rejects the ideas of the Leader of mankind. He repulses him and thinks: 'I will know nothing of thee, who wouldst guide the kernel of my being into future incarnations where mankind will be outwardly more perfect. I wish to be united with my present form.' A person who thrusts from him such a Leader of mankind will appear again in the same form. And if this attitude hardens, then he will also thrust from him the

Leader in the next incarnation. He will appear again and again as the same figure.

We shall now picture those who listen to the great Leader of humanity. They will preserve the soul with its eternal life-kernel. Mankind will have gone forward but they too will appear in an ever progressed form. He, however, who thrusts the Leader of humanity from him must reappear again and again in the same way. That is the legend of Ahasuerus, who has thrust from him the Christ, the Leader of humanity. Man has either hardened or possesses the possibility of developing to higher stages. Races would not stay behind and become decadent if there were not people who wish to stay behind and are obliged to stay behind, since they have not developed their eternal life-kernel. Older races only persist because there are people who cannot or will not move forward to a higher racial form. I cannot today speak about the whole series of possibilities, in the course of earthly evolution, for man to become one with the race, to grow together with what is the character of one race or another. Think of the Atlantean race; souls have gone through it, but not all have passed out of it. There are 16 possibilities of becoming merged with the race. They are called the '16 paths of perdition'. On these paths man would merge with the material. By striving forward, however, he is drawn up from race to race to ever higher stages.

We see then that it is actually possible for a person to combine with the one incarnation in such a way that he remains behind in evolution. His other soul-brothers are therefore at a higher stage when he reappears in a new incarnation. He must then content himself with an inferior incarnation which has been left to him in a decadent race. This is something that positively takes place. It need not frighten people, however, for the present phase of evolution. No one is obliged to take all the 16 paths and thereby fall out of evolution. We must only be aware of the possibility.

Now let us take an extreme case and imagine that a person unites too fully with what is to constitute the character of an incarnation. Let us suppose he reaches what is to be reached in 16 incarnations; he takes the 16 false paths. The earth does not wait for him, the earth goes forward and he finally arrives at a point where he can no longer incorporate in a human body, for none are in existence. There will be no more bodies in which souls that have grown too much involved in their bodily nature can incarnate. Such souls lose the possibility of incarnation and find no other opportunity. Just think what they will have lost. It is possible, but only in exceptional cases, that even during earth evolution souls will be unable to incarnate because there are no more bodies bad enough. These people have gone so far that they have no other opportunity of incarnating in the normal course of evolution. Let us suppose such beings should remain on the earth – it will only be single cases. And now, since the later is the fruit of the earlier, these would then find no bodies suitable for them. They are, as it were, too good for the bodies of a subordinate order and for the other bodies they are too bad. They must therefore live a bodiless existence. They must cut themselves off entirely from the progress of evolution. Why have they deserved this? By reason of the fact that they have not made use of life! The world is around them; they have possessed senses in order to perceive the world, to enrich the life-kernel and mould it to a higher stage. They do not advance with world evolution, they remain behind at a certain stage. Beings that stay behind at such stages appear in a later epoch with approximately the character of the earlier age. They have grown together with it, but not in the forms of the later epoch. They appear in a later epoch as subordinate nature spirits. In fact the human race will furnish a whole number of such new nature spirits in the second half of the Jupiter evolution, for man will have fully completed the fifth principle at the Jupiter stage. For those who have not used the opportunity on earth to develop the fifth principle, there will be no available form. They will appear as nature spirits, and they will appear then with four principles, the fourth being the highest. Whereas the normally advanced man will have the principles 5, 4, 3, 2 at the Jupiter stage, these people will have 4, 3, 2, 1. That would be the destiny of those who have not gradually developed their higher principles by making use of earthly life. They become nature spirits, so to speak, of future evolutionary periods, working invisibly. Just the same occurred in the case of our present nature spirits in the earlier periods of evolution, except in so far as there are, of course, continual changes according to the character of the different periods. Everything has now been graded, so to speak, according to moral responsibility, and because this is so, the nature spirits that arise from the human race will have a certain morality. Upon Jupiter there will be nature spirits which have moral responsibility.

Let us now recollect what I have said as to how Jupiter differs from our Earth. We have described the nature of the Earth as that of the planet of love, in contrast to the nature of the Old Moon, the planet of wisdom. As love has evolved on Earth so did the wisdom that we find all around us evolve on the Moon. Love in its lowest form originated in the ancient Lemurian age and becomes transformed to ever higher stages up to the highest spiritual form. When in the future the Earth planet appears as Jupiter, the Jupiter dwellers will direct their gaze upon love as people on Earth do upon wisdom. We observe the thigh bone into which wisdom is woven; the whole Earth is in a certain sense crystallized wisdom, which was formed little by little on the Moon. But wisdom was formed gradually just as on our Earth love is gradually formed. And just as we wonder at the wisdom in all that surrounds us, so he who will one day inhabit Jupiter will feel wafting towards him the love that will lie in all things. This love will stream forth from all beings and speak to us, as the wisdom speaks to us which is secreted into the Earth through the Old Moon existence.

Thus the cosmos moves forward from stage to stage. The Earth is the cosmos of love, and every condition has its special task. As a common wisdom prevails throughout our Earth, so will a common love prevail throughout Jupiter. And as the destructive forces of wisdom originate from those beings who stayed behind on the Moon, so there will appear upon Jupiter the destructive forces of love from beings who have remained behind. Into the midst of the general tapestry of the Jupiter existence will be set the hideous forms of the retarded beings with egoistic demands for love, and they will be the mighty devastating powers in the Jupiter existence. The staying behind of human beings in individual incarnations creates the destructive nature-powers on Jupiter. Thus we see how the world is woven, harmful elements as well as beneficent; we have a moral element woven into the world process.

The following table shows all the forms of nature spirits:

	Physical body and above	Below
Gnomes	1	3
Undines	2	2
Sylphs	3	1
Salamanders	4	0

Thus the gnomes have three principles below and one above, the undines have two principles below and two above, the sylphs have one below and three above. They are all retarded beings which surge through the figure and form of the earth as elemental beings. They have not been able to attain to a spirit; they consist purely of body and soul. Gnomes, undines and sylphs are two-membered beings.

Now you will ask me where the salamanders really come from. They are actually a fourth kind. If you ask – I can only indicate this in conclusion – whence come these three kinds, gnomes, sylphs, undines, I can only answer that they are beings which have remained behind. But the salamanders in a certain way are human, since they have partially developed the fourth principle. They are not advanced enough, however, to be able to assume human shape. Where does this fourth species come from? I will explain this in conclusion. When you understand this you will be able to understand many of the secrets of surrounding nature. You know that when we trace man back in his evolution we come to more and more spiritual forms. Man has progressed little by little to physical existence. We know that the different animal species have been gradually ejected, so to speak, as the retarded brethren of the advancing human evolution. Man attained such advanced development by being the last of all to take a physical form. The other animal creatures are at a backward stage because they were not able to wait, because they pressed into the earthly organs and physical organization earlier. But the animals have group souls which work into the physical world though they exist only on the astral plane. We see the wisdom given by the Moon to our evolution most comprehensively developed in the animal kingdom by the group souls. Man creates his civilization *through wisdom*, but he must not ascribe wisdom to himself. Any human wisdom is not merely in man, but is present in a far more comprehensive way in our whole earth planet. One who sets great store by mankind may say: 'What strides humanity has made in wisdom! The recent inventions for instance are a witness to it.' And now think of your school days and the principal discoveries that were told us then. Perhaps you will also remember the discovery of paper. Human wisdom got to the stage of inventing paper. It was certainly an achievement of human wisdom.

But the wasp knew it much earlier still! You all know wasps' nests. They are made of the same substance as the paper made by man. We could go through all nature and we should find ruling wisdom everywhere. How much earlier than man the wasp spirit discovered paper! The individual wasp does not do it, it is the group ego.

So we see that what constitutes human wisdom is interwoven and impressed into the whole earth. But the relation of the animal to its group soul is only up to a certain point what it actually ought to be from the cosmic standpoint – if I may say so. What is this relation of the group soul to the single animal? Take perhaps the group soul of an insect species. When the single insect dies it is exactly the same for the group soul as when you lose a hair and another grows. The animal forms that come into being are only fresh creations of the group soul. You can follow up the animal ranks for a long way and everywhere you will find that what is on the physical plane has just the same action as a cloud dissolving and reforming. The group spirit is metamorphosed and its physical members merely renew themselves. That happens however only up to a certain stage, after which something else takes place in the animal kingdom. This is very important just when you come to the so-called higher animals. Precisely there something occurs which no longer seems quite to fit in with what I have been describing.

Let us take as a marked case the apes. The ape, for instance, brings too much from the group soul down into its own individual existence. Whereas in the relatively lower animal the whole physical form goes back into the group soul, the ape keeps something in the physical organization which cannot go back. What the ape detaches from the group spirit can no longer return. So too in the case of man, you have the ego which goes from incarnation to incarnation and is capable through development of reaching our different stages. Here too there is no possibility of returning into the group spirit. The ape has something which is similar to the human ego.

A whole series of animals draws too much out of the group soul, others again draw something out in another way. And this remains in our evolution and works as the fourth class of elemental spirits. They are detached group souls of animals whose individual souls cannot return into the group soul, because they have carried their development beyond the normal point. From countless animals such ego-like beings remain behind. They are called salamanders. That is the highest form, for they are ego-like.

With these remarks I have introduced you to the nature of a series of beings which we shall learn to know more exactly, for today we have only learnt their kind of existence and connections. But they work in a certain way in our world. The classification can in fact give but little; in the course of time, however, we shall come as well to their description. These salamander-like beings come about even today in a strange manner, when certain human natures of specially low order, who nevertheless will certainly incarnate again, leave behind a part of their lower nature. There are such people. No human being today, of course, can be so evil that he falls completely out of evolution, but he can leave part of his nature behind. These are then especially harmful elements within our evolution – these partially detached human natures which have remained as a species of spirit and permeate our existence. Much of what interpenetrates our spiritual space and of which we have not the least idea shows itself only too well in external phenomena. Many bad things in civilization which today seem natural will only be explained when people know with what disturbing, retarding forces they have to do. The effects will be evident in many decadent phenomena of our civilization. It is only because this is foreseen by those who know how to read the signs of the time, that the Anthroposophical Movement has been called into existence. One who stands in the world without knowledge has to let things work upon him. One who has insight, however, will be in a position to keep man free from the disturbing influences of these beings.

If you ponder this in the right way, the deep spirituality and healing nature of the Anthroposophical Movement will be seen. Its aim is to free man from the forces that want to hold him back. We should fall completely into decadence if we were unwilling to concern ourselves with knowledge of these things. You will experience all sorts of cross cultural phenomena in the near future. You will find that those

standing within them will look upon those people as
dreamers who call things by their right names. The world has
reached the stage where those who know reality are called
dreamers and visionaries, whereas the real visionaries are
those who wish to cling only to the external. The progress of
civilization rests upon man's penetrating with knowledge
into the character of the hostile powers. Knowledge, when
understood in the sense often expressed here, is something
that will, from the anthroposophical spiritual stream, bring a
certain saying to true realization. It is the saying which we
have learnt in Christian esotericism, and which the Leader
of Christian life proclaimed to His followers: 'Ye shall know
the truth and the truth shall make you free.'[21] Knowledge of
full and complete truth and reality can make man free, and
wholly and entirely human.

V. Phantoms, Spectres and Demons

Berlin, 4 June 1908

IN THE last lecture we were particularly occupied with the presence of all sorts of spiritual beings which are to be found, so to speak, between the sense-perceptible kingdoms of nature that surround us. We saw especially how in the place where the beings of different nature-kingdoms come together, where the plant is pressed close to the stone at a spring, where ordinary stone impinges on a metal as constantly occurs under the earth, where there is a communion as between bee and blossom, how everywhere in such places forces are developed which draw various beings, whom we have called elemental beings, into earthly existence. Moreover, in connection with these elemental beings we have been occupied with the fact of a certain cutting off, a detaching of beings from their whole connection. We have seen that the elemental beings called by spiritual science 'Salamanders' have in part their origin from detached parts of animal group souls. These have, as it were, ventured too far forward into our physical world and have not been able to find their way back and unite again with the group soul, after the death and dissolution of the animal. We know that in the regular course of our life the beings of our earth, the beings of the animal, plant and mineral kingdoms, have their 'ego soul' – if one may so call it – have indeed such ego souls as man, differing only in the fact that the ego souls of other beings are in other worlds. We know that man is that being in our cycle of evolution who has an individual ego here on the physical plane – at least during his waking life. We know further that the beings which we call animals are so conditioned that – speaking loosely – similarly-formed animals have a group soul or group ego which is in the so-called astral world. Further, the beings which we call plants have a dreamless sleeping consciousness for the physical world here but they have group egos which dwell in the lower parts of the devachanic world; and, finally, the stones, the minerals, have their group egos in the higher parts of Devachan. One who moves clairvoyantly in the astral and devachanic worlds has intercourse there with the group souls of the animals, plants and minerals in the same way as here in the physical world he has intercourse during the day with other human souls or egos.

Now we must be clear that in many ways man is a very complicated being – we have often spoken of this complexity in different lectures. But he will appear more and more complicated the further we go into the connections with great cosmic facts. In order to realize that man is not quite the simple being which he may perhaps appear to a naive observation we need only remember that by night, from going to sleep to waking up, the human being of the present evolutionary cycle is quite a different being from what he is by day. His physical and etheric bodies lie in bed and the ego with the astral body is lifted out of them. Let us consider both conditions, and in the first place the physical and etheric bodies. They lie there, and if we disregard the transitional state of dream they have what we may call a sleep consciousness devoid of content, perceptions or dreams. But the ego and the astral body outside have, in this present cycle of evolution, just the same dreamless sleep consciousness. The sleeping human being, whether in the members remaining here in the physical world or in those which are in the astral world, has the same consciousness as the plant covering of the earth. We must occupy ourselves a little with these two separated parts of the sleeping human being.

From other lectures we know that the human being of the present time has arisen slowly and gradually. We know that he received the first rudiments of a physical body in the embodiment of our Earth lying in a primeval past which we call the Saturn evolution. We know that then in a second embodiment of our Earth, the Sun evolution, he received the etheric or life body; that in the third embodiment, the Moon evolution, he also received the astral body, and that in the present Earth embodiment of our planet he acquired what we call the ego. Thus the human being has evolved quite slowly and gradually. This physical body which man bears today is actually his oldest part, the part that has gone through most metamorphoses. It has undergone four changes. The first rudiment, received by man on Old Saturn, has gone through three modifications, on the Sun, on the Moon, and finally on the Earth, and is expressed in man's present sense-organs. They were quite different organs on Old Saturn, but their first rudiments were there while no other part of the physical body as yet existed. We can look on Old Saturn as a single being, entirely consisting of sense-organs. On the Sun the etheric body was added, the physical body went through a change, and the organs arose which we call today the glands, though at first they existed merely in their rudiments. Then on the Moon, when the physical body had undergone a third transformation through the impress of the astral body, were added those organs which we know as the nerve organs. And finally on the Earth was added the present blood-system, the expression of the ego, as the nervous system is the expression of the astral body, the glandular system of the etheric body, and the senses system the physical expression of the physical body itself. We have seen in former lectures that the blood system appeared for the first time in our Earth evolution and we ask: Why does blood flow in the present form in the blood channels? What does this blood express? Blood is the expression of the ego and with this we will consider a possible misunderstanding, namely, that man actually misunderstands the present physical human body.

The human body as it is today is only one form of many. On the Moon, on the Sun, on Saturn, it was there but always different. On the Moon, for instance, there was as yet no mineral kingdom, on the Sun there was no plant world in our sense, and on Saturn no animal kingdom – there was solely the human being in his first physical rudiments. Now when we reflect on this we must be clear that the present human body is not only physical body, but physical-mineral body, and that to the laws of the physical world – hence it is the 'physical body' – it has assimilated the laws and substances of the mineral kingdom, which permeate it today. On the Moon the physical human body had not yet assimilated those laws: if one had burnt it there would have been no ash, for there were no minerals in the present earthly sense. Let us remember that to be physical and to be mineral are two quite different things. The human body is physical because it is governed by the same laws as the stone; it is at the same time mineral because it has been impregnated with mineral substances. The first germ of the physical body was present on Saturn, but there were no solid bodies, no water, no gases. On Saturn there was nothing at all but a condition of warmth. The modern physicist knows of no such condition because he thinks that warmth can only appear in connection with gases, water or solid objects. But that is an error. The physical body which today has assimilated the mineral kingdom was on Old Saturn a nexus of physical laws. We are physical laws working in lines, in forms, which you learn to know as laws in physics. Externally the physical human being was manifested on Saturn purely as a being which lived in warmth. We must thus clearly distinguish between the mineral element and the actual physical principle of man's body. It is physical law which governs the physical body. It belongs, for example, to the physical principle that our ear has such a form, that it receives sound in quite a definite way; to the mineral nature of the ear belong the substances which are impregnated into this scaffolding of physical laws.

Now that we have become clear about this and realize particularly how the sense-organs, glands, nerves and blood are the expressions of our fourfold nature, let us turn again to the observation of the sleeping human being. When man is asleep the physical and etheric bodies lie on the bed, the astral body and the ego are outside. But now let us remember that the astral body is the principle of the nervous system and the ego that of the blood system. Thus during the night the astral body has deserted that part of the physical body of which, so to say, it is the cause, namely, the nervous system. For only when the astral body became part of man on the Moon could the nervous system arise. Thus the astral body callously leaves what belongs to it, what it is actually due to maintain, and in the same way the ego deserts that which it has called into life. The principles of the blood and of the astral body are outside and the sleeping physical and etheric bodies are absolutely alone. But now nothing of a material physical nature can subsist in the form which has been called forth by a spiritual principle when this spiritual principle is no longer there. That is quite out of the question. Never can a nervous system live unless astral beings are active in it, and never can a blood system live unless ego-beings are active in it. Thus in the night you all meanly desert your nervous and blood systems and relinquish them to other beings of an astral nature. Beings which are of the same nature as your ego now descend into your organism. Every night the human organism is occupied by beings fitted to maintain it. The physical body and the etheric body which lie on the bed are at the same time interpenetrated by these astral and ego beings; they are actually within the physical body. We might call them intruders, but that is in no sense correct. We ought in many ways to call them guardian spirits, for they are the sustainers of what man callously deserts in the night.

Now it is not so bad for man to leave his bodies every night. I have already said that the astral body and the ego are perpetually active in the night. They rid the physical body of the wear and tear which the day has given, which in a broad sense we call fatigue. Man is refreshed and renewed in the morning because during the night his astral body and ego have removed the fatigue which were given him by the impressions of daily life. This all-night activity of the astral body in getting rid of the fatigue substances is a definite fact to clairvoyant perception. The ego and astral body work from outside on the physical and etheric bodies. But in the present cycle of his evolution man is not yet advanced enough to be able to carry out such an activity quite independently. He can only do so under the guidance of other, higher beings. So the human being is taken every night into the bosom of higher beings, as it were, and they endow him with the power of working in the right way on his physical and etheric bodies. These at the same time are the beings – that is why we may not call them intruders – who care for man's blood and nerve systems in the right way in the night.

As long as no abnormalities arise, the co-operation of spiritual beings with man is justified. But such irregularities can very well enter, and here we come to a chapter of spiritual science which is extraordinarily important for the practical life of the human soul. One would like it to be known in the widest circles, and not only theoretically, but as giving the foundation for certain activities of the human soul life. It is not generally imagined that the facts of the soul life have a far-reaching effect. In certain connections I have also called your attention to the fact that it is only when viewed in the light of spiritual science that events in the life of the soul can find their true explanation. We all know the deep significance of the statement: 'Regarded from the spiritual-scientific aspect a lie is a kind of murder.' I have explained that a sort of explosion really takes place in the astral world when a person utters a lie – even, in a certain way, if he only thinks it. Something takes place in the spiritual world when a person lies, which has a far more devastating effect for that world than any misfortune in the physical world. But things which one relates at a certain stage of spiritual-scientific observation, characterizing them as far as is possible then, gain more and more clearness and confirmation when one advances in the knowledge of spiritual science.

Today we shall learn of another effect of lying, slandering, although these words are not used here in the ordinary crude sense. When more subtly, out of convention, for instance, or out of all sorts of social or party considerations, people colour the truth, we there have to do with a lie in the sense of spiritual science. In many respects man's whole life is saturated, if not with lies, yet with manifestations bearing an untruthful colouring. The enlightened materialist can at any rate see that an impression is made on his physical body if he receives a blow on the skull from an axe, or if his head is cut off by the railway, or he has an ulcer somewhere or is attacked by bacilli. He will then admit that effects are produced on the physical body. What is not usually considered at all is that man is a spiritual unity, that what happens in his higher members, the astral body and ego, has an actual effect right down into his physical nature. It is not considered, for instance, that the uttering of lies and untruthfulness, untruth even in the affairs of life, has a definite effect on the human physical body. Spiritual vision can experience the following. If a person, let us say, has told a lie during the day, its effect remains in the physical body and is to be seen by clairvoyant perception while the person sleeps. Let us suppose this person is altogether untruthful, piling up lies, then he will have many such effects in his physical body. All this hardens, as it were, in the night, and then something very important happens. These hardenings, these 'enclosures', in the physical body are not at all agreeable to the beings who from higher worlds must take possession of the physical body in the night and carry out the functions otherwise exercised by the astral body and ego. The result is that in the course of life and by reason of a body diseased, one might say, through lies, portions of those beings who descend into man at night become detached. Here we have again detachment processes and they lead to the fact that when a man dies his physical body does not merely follow the paths which it would normally take. Certain beings are left behind, beings which have been created in the physical body through the effect of lying and slander, and have been detached from the spiritual world. Such beings, detached in this circuitous way, now flit and whirr about in our world and belong to the class that we call 'phantoms'. They form a certain group of elemental beings related to our physical body and invisible to physical sight. They multiply through lies and calumnies, and these in actual fact populate our earthly globe with phantoms. In this way we learn to know a new class of elemental beings.

But now not only lies and slanders but also other things belonging to the soul life produce an effect on the human body. It is lies and slanders which so act on the physical body that a detaching of phantoms is caused. Other things again work in a similar way on the etheric body. You must not be amazed at such phenomena of the soul; in spiritual life one must be able to take things with all calmness. Matters, for example, which have a harmful result on the etheric body are bad laws, or bad social measures prevailing in a community. All that leads to want of harmony, all that makes for bad adjustments between people, works in such a way through the feeling which it creates in the common life that the effect is continued into the etheric body. The accumulation in the etheric body caused through these experiences of the soul again brings about detachments from the beings working in from the spiritual worlds and these likewise are now to be found in our environment – they are 'spectres' or 'ghosts'. Thus these beings that exist in the etheric world, the life world, we see grow out of the life of human beings. Many a person can go about amongst us and for one who is able to see these things spiritually, his physical body is crammed, one might say, with phantoms, his etheric body crammed with spectres, and as a rule after a person's death or shortly afterwards all this rises up and disperses and populates the world.

So we see how subtly the spiritual events of our life are continued, how lies, calumnies, bad social arrangements, deposit their creations spiritually among us on our earth. But now you can also understand that if in normal daily life the physical body, etheric body, astral body and ego belong together, and the physical body and etheric body have to let other beings press in and act upon them, then the astral body and the ego are not in a normal condition either. At any rate they are in a somewhat different position as regards the physical and etheric bodies. These two have in sleeping man the consciousness of the plants. But the plants on the other hand have their ego above in Devachan. Hence the physical and etheric bodies of sleeping man must likewise be sustained by beings which unfold their consciousness from Devachan. Now it is true that man's astral body and ego are in a higher world, but he himself also sleeps dreamlessly like the plants. That the plants have only a physical and an etheric body and that man in his sleeping condition possesses further an astral body and ego makes no difference as regards the plant-nature. True, man has been drawn upwards into the spiritual, the astral world, but not yet high enough upwards with his ego to justify the sleep-condition. The consequence is that beings must now enter his astral body too when the human being goes to sleep. And so it is: influences from the devachanic world press all the time into man's astral body. They need not in the least be abnormal influences; they may come from what we call man's higher ego. For we know that man is gradually rising to the devachanic world, inasmuch as he approaches ever nearer to a state of spiritualization, and what is being prepared there sends its influences into him today when he sleeps. But there are not merely these normal influences. This would simply and solely be the case if human beings were fully to understand what it is to value and esteem the freedom of another. Mankind at present is still very far removed from that. Think only how the modern man for the most part wants to overrule the mind of another, how he cannot bear someone else to think and like differently, how he wants to work upon the other's soul. In all that works from soul to soul in our world, from the giving of unjustifiable advice to all those methods which people employ in order to overwhelm others, in every act that does not allow the free soul to confront the free soul but employs even in the slightest degree forcible means of convincing and persuasion, in all this forces are working from soul to soul which again so influence these souls that it is expressed in the night in the astral body. The astral body gets those 'enclosures' and thereby beings are detached from other worlds and whirr through our world again as elemental beings. They belong to the class of demons. Their existence is solely due to the fact that intolerance and oppression of thought have in various ways been used in our world. That is how these hosts of demons have arisen in our world. Thus we have learnt again today to know of beings which are just as real as the things which we perceive through our physical senses, and which very definitely produce effects in human life. Humanity would have advanced quite differently if intolerance had not created the demons which pervade our world, influencing people continually. They are at the same time spirits of prejudice. One understands the intricacies of life when one learns about these entanglements between the spiritual world in the higher sense and our human world. All these beings, as we have said, are there, and they whizz and whirr through the world in which we live.

Now let us remember something else which has also been said before. We have pointed out that in the human being of the last third of the Atlantean age, before the Atlantean flood, the relation of etheric body to physical body was quite different from what it had been earlier. Today the physical part of the head and the etheric part practically coincide. That was quite different in ancient Atlantis; there we have the etheric part of the head projecting far out, especially in the region of the forehead. We now have a central point for the etheric and physical parts approximately between the eyebrows. These two parts came together in the last third of the Atlantean age and today they coincide. Thereby man is able to say 'I' to himself and feel an independent personality. Thus the etheric and physical bodies of the head have joined together. This has come about so that man could become the sense being that he is within our physical world, so that he can enrich his inner life through what he takes in through sense impressions, through smell, taste, sight, and so on. All of this becomes embodied in his inner being, so that having obtained it he can use it for the further development of the whole cosmos. What he thus acquires can be acquired in no other way, and therefore we have always said we must not take spiritual science in an ascetic sense, as a flight from the physical world. All that happens here is taken with us out of the physical world and it would be lost to the spiritual world if it were not collected here first.

But humanity is now getting nearer and nearer to a new condition. In this post-Atlantean age we have gone through various culture epochs: the old Indian, the ancient Persian, lying before the time of Zarathustra, then the epoch which we have called the Babylonian-Assyrian-Chaldean-Egyptian, then the Graeco-Latin, and now we stand in the fifth culture-epoch of the post-Atlantean age. Ours will be followed by a sixth and a seventh epoch. Whereas in the course of past ages and up to our own time the united structure of our etheric and physical bodies has always grown firmer, more closely united inwardly, man is approaching a period in the future when the etheric body gradually loosens itself again and becomes independent. The way back is taken. There are people today who have a much looser etheric body than others. This loosening of the etheric body is only right for man if during his different incarnations in those culture-epochs he has absorbed so much into himself that when his etheric body goes out again it will take with it the right fruits from the physical sense world of the earth, fruits suitable for incorporation into the increasingly independent etheric body. The more spiritual are the concepts which man finds within the physical world, the more he takes with him in his etheric body. All the utilitarian ideas, all the concepts bound up with machine and industry which only serve outer needs and the outer life, and which man absorbs in our present earthly existence, are unsuitable for incorporation in the etheric body. But all the concepts he absorbs of the artistic, the beautiful, the religious – and everything can be immersed in the sphere of wisdom, art, religion – all this endows man's etheric body with the capability and possibility of being organized independently. Since this can be seen in advance, it has often been emphasized here that the world-conception of spiritual science must send its impulses and activities into practical life. Spiritual science must never remain a conversational subject for tea-parties or any other pursuit apart from ordinary life; it must work its way into the whole of our civilization. If spiritual-scientific thoughts are one day understood, then people will understand that everything our age accomplishes must be permeated by spiritual principles. Many human beings, among them Richard Wagner, foresaw in certain fields such a penetration with spiritual principles. Some day people will understand how to build a railway station so that it streams out truth like a temple and is in fact simply an expression suited to what is within it. There is still very much to do. These impulses therefore must be effective and they will be effective when spiritual-scientific thoughts are more fully understood.

I still have a vivid recollection of a rectorial address given about 25 years ago by a well-known architect.[22] He spoke about style in architecture and uttered the remarkable sentence: 'Architectural styles are not invented, they grow out of the spiritual life!' At the same time he showed why our age, if indeed it produces architectural styles, only revives old ones and is incapable of finding a new style because it has as yet no inner spiritual life. When the world creates spiritual life again then all will be possible. Then we shall feel that the human soul shines towards us from all we look at, just as in the Middle Ages every lock on a door expressed what man's soul understood of outer forms. Spiritual science will not be understood till it meets us everywhere in this way as if crystallized in forms. But then mankind too will live as spirit in the spirit. Then, however, man will be preparing more and more something that he takes with him when he again rises into the spiritual world, when his etheric body becomes self-dependent. Thus must people immerse themselves in the spiritual world if evolution is to go further in the right way.

Nothing symbolizes the permeation of the world with the spirit so beautifully as the story of the miracle of Pentecost. When you contemplate it, it is as though the interpenetration of the world with spiritual life were indicated prophetically through the descent of the 'fiery tongues'.[23] Everything must be given life again through the spirit; that abstract intellectual relation which man has to the yearly festivals must also become concrete and living again. Now, at this time of Pentecost, Whitsuntide, let us try to occupy our souls with the thoughts that can proceed from today's lecture. Then the festival, which as we know is established on a spiritual foundation, will again signify something living for man when his etheric body is ripe for spiritual creation. But if man does not absorb the Whitsuntide spirit, then the etheric body goes out of the physical body and is far too weak to overcome what has already been created, those worlds of spectres, phantoms, demons, which the world creates as phenomena existing at its side.

VI. Elemental Spirits of Birth and Death

Dornach, 6 October 1917

As I have said in my earlier lectures, the time has come for humanity to know certain truths concerning the spiritual background to the physical world. If people are not going to be prepared to accept these truths out of their own good will, they will be forced to learn them from the terrible events that will happen as time goes on.

The question may arise as to why now is the time for humanity to learn these truths, some of which are liable to shock people. They have of course existed for a long time, but humanity in general was protected and did not have to accept them. Many of these truths were carefully guarded in the ancient Mysteries, as you know, so that people in the surrounding areas were not exposed to the disturbing effect of these truths. Now, we have often said that it is fear of the great truths that prevents people from accepting them. Those who have this fear today – and there are indeed many of them – could of course say:' Why cannot humanity go on in a kind of sleep state where these truths are concerned? As it is, people have grown tense and fearful in recent times, and why should they be exposed to those great and fearsome truths?'

Let us go into this question, first of all considering why from now on humanity has to be treated differently, as it were, by the world of the spirit than has been the case so far in this post-Atlantean age.

In my earlier lectures I spoke of the non-physical world which borders directly on our physical world. This is the world humanity will need to know about in the time which lies just ahead. You know, as soon as you enter into a non-physical world, everything is different from the way it is here. You get to know certain entities, and above all things of a special nature which are hidden from the sight of weak humanity – 'sight' here includes anything conveyed in insights and ideas. Why has the human eye been deflected from this other world in the post-Atlantean age, right up to the present moment? It is because there are entities in this next-door world – other, higher worlds lie beyond it – which could only be made known to human beings under certain conditions. They have a specific function in the whole universe and especially also in human evolution. There are many different kinds of these entities in the other region.

Today I want to talk to you about one class of such entities, the class whose function in the great scheme of things is connected with human birth and death. You should never believe that human birth and death are actually as they present themselves to the senses. Spiritual entities are in-volved when a human being enters this physical world from the non-physical, and then leaves it again for the non-physical world. To give them a name, let us call them the 'elemental spirits of birth and death' for the moment. It is true that the individuals who until now were initiated in the Mysteries considered it to be their strict duty not to speak to people in general of these elemental spirits of birth and death. If one were to speak of them, and of the whole way in which these elemental spirits live, one would be speaking of something that would seem like red-hot coals to people, for this is how humanity has developed in the post-Atlantean age. We might also use another analogy. If people get to know more about the essential nature of these elemental spirits of birth and death and do so in full consciousness, they come to know powers which are inimical to life in the physical world.

Anyone with more or less normal feelings, even today, will be shaken to learn the truth that in order to bring about birth and death in the physical world, the divine spirits who guide world destinies have to use elemental spirits who actually are the enemies of everything human beings seek and desire for

their welfare and well-being here in the physical world. If
everything was done just to suit the wishes of human beings
– to be comfortable in this physical world, be fit and well as
we go to sleep and wake up again and go about our work – if
all spirits were of a kind to see to it that we have such a
comfortable life, birth and death could not be. To bring about
birth and death the gods need entities whose minds and whole
way of looking at the world give them the urge to destroy and
lay waste to everything which provides for the welfare of
human beings here in the physical world.

We have to get used to the idea that the world is not made
as people would really like it to be and that there exists the
element which in the Egyptian Mysteries was known as 'iron
necessity'. As part of this iron necessity, entities hostile to the
physical world are used by the gods to bring about birth and
death for human beings.

So we are looking at a world that is immediately next
to our own, a world that day by day, hour by hour, has to do
with our own world, for the processes of birth and death
happen every day and every hour here on earth. The moment
human beings cross the threshold to the other world they
enter into a sphere where entities live and are active whose
whole conduct, views and desires are destructive for
ordinary physical human life. If this had been made known
to people outside the Mysteries before now, if people had
been given an idea of these entities, the following would
inevitably have happened. If people who are quite unable to
deal with their instincts and drives, with their passions, had
known that destructive entities were present around them all
the time, they would have used the powers of those destructive entities. They would not have used them the way the gods
do in birth and death, however, but within the realm of
physical life. If people had felt the desire to be destructive in
some sphere or other, they would have had ample opportunity to make these entities serve them, for it is easy to make
them serve us. This truth was kept hidden to protect ordinary

life from the destructive elemental spirits of birth and death. The question is, should we not continue to keep them hidden? This is not possible, and for quite specific reasons, one of which is connected with a great, important cosmic law. I could give you a general formula, but it will be better to use the actual form it is taking now and in the immediate future to demonstrate this law to you. As you know, not long ago growing numbers of impulses came into human evolution which did not exist before and which are quite characteristic of our present civilization. Try and go back in your mind to times not very long ago. You will find times when there were no steam locomotives, when people did not yet use electricity as we do now – times perhaps when only thinkers like Leonardo da Vinci were able to have the idea, theoretically and on the basis of experiments, that humans could create apparatus which would enable them to fly.[24] All this has come to realization in a relatively short time. Just consider how much depends on the use of steam, of electricity, of the changes in atmospheric density which has made airships possible, or the knowledge of statics which has led to the aeroplane. Consider everything which has come into human evolution in recent times. Think of the destructive powers of dynamite, etc., and you can easily imagine, seeing how swiftly this has happened, that new and different fabulous things of this kind will be the goal of future human endeavour. I think you can easily see that the ideal for the near future will be to have not more and more Goethes, but more and more Edisons. This really is the ideal of modern humanity.

Modern people do, of course, believe that all this – the telegraph, telephones, the use of steam power, etc. – happens without the participation of spiritual entities. This is not the case, however. The development of human civilization involves the participation of elemental spirits, even if people do not know about it. Modern materialists imagine that the telephone and telegraph, and the steam engines driven long distances and also used by farmers, have been constructed merely on the basis of what people produce by the sweat of their brow. Everything people do in this respect is under the influence of elemental spirits. They are always involved and helping us in this. People are not taking the initiative on their own in this field – they are guided. In laboratories, workshops, really everywhere where the spirit of invention is active, elemental spirits are providing the inspiration.

The elemental spirits who have given impulses to our civilization from the eighteenth century onwards are of the same kind as those used by the gods to bring about birth and death. This is one of the mysteries which human beings have to discover today. And the law of world history of which I have spoken is that as evolution proceeds the gods always rule for a time within a particular sphere of elemental spirits and then human beings enter into this same sphere and use the elemental spirits. In earlier times, the elemental spirits of birth and death essentially served the divine spirits who guided the world; since our day – and this has been going on for some time now – the elemental spirits of birth and death are serving technology, industry and human commerce. It is important to let this disturbing truth enter into our souls with all its power and intensity.

Something is happening in this fifth post-Atlantean period of civilization which is similar to something that happened in Atlantean times, during the fourth Atlantean period. I have spoken of this before. Up to the fourth Atlantean period the divine spirits who guide human evolution used certain elemental spirits. They had to use them because not only birth and death had to be brought about at that time but also something else, which may be said to be closer to the earth. You will remember some of the descriptions I have given of the Atlantean age, when human beings were still flexible in their physical nature and their souls could make their bodies grow large or remain dwarf-like, with their outer appearance depending on their inner nature. Please call this to mind again.[25] Today the service that certain elemental spirits give to the divine spirits on occasions of birth and death is clearly apparent in physical terms. In those times, when outer appearance was in accord with inner nature, certain elemental spirits were serving the gods for the whole of human life. When the Atlantean age had reached its fourth period, people again began to rule the elemental spirits, which had previously been used by the gods, to govern the growth and general physiognomy of human beings. Human beings gained control of certain divine powers and made use of them.

The consequence was that from about the middle of the Atlantean age it was possible for individuals who desired to harm their fellow human beings to use all kinds of creative powers on them – keeping them dwarf-sized in growth or making them into giants, or letting the physical organism develop in such a way that the individual concerned would be an intelligent person or a cretin. A terrible power was in human hands in the middle of the Atlantean age. You know, for I have drawn attention to this, that this was not kept secret, though not from any kind of evil intent. According to one of the laws of world history, something which initially was the work of the gods had to become the work of human beings. This led to serious mischief in the Atlantean age, so that over the last three or four periods of civilization the whole of Atlantean civilization had to be guided towards its own destruction. Our own civilization was saved and brought across from Atlantis, as I have described elsewhere, and you will recall my descriptions of what happened in the Atlantean age.

In the last three, or two, periods of post-Atlantean civilization in the fifth stage of earth evolution, work now done by the gods will again become work to be done by humanity. We are only in the early stages of the technological, industrial and commercial activities which proceed under the influence of the elemental spirits of birth and death. This influence and its effects will be increasingly more radical. Until now, the elemental spirits of birth and death have been guided by the gods, and their influence has been limited to the coming into being and passing away of humans at the physical level. But the civilization of our own and future ages has to be such that these spirits can be active in technology, industry, commerce, and so on.

There is also another, quite specific, aspect to this. As I have said, these elemental spirits are the enemies of human welfare and want to destroy it. We have to see things straight and not have any illusions concerning the radical nature of this. Civilization must progress in the fields of technology, industry and commerce. But by its very nature such a civilization cannot serve the well-being of humanity in the physical world; it can only prove destructive to the human weal.

This will be an unpalatable truth for people who never tire of making great speeches on the tremendous advances made in modern civilization, for they see things in abstract terms and know nothing of the rise and fall which is part of human evolution. I have made brief reference to the causes of destruction in Atlantis. The commercial, industrial and technological civilization which is now in its beginnings harbours elements which will lead to the decline and fall of the fifth earth period. And we only see things straight, and face reality, if we admit that we are here beginning to work on something which must lead to catastrophe.

This is what it means to enter into iron necessity. Looking for an easy way out people might say: 'All right, I won't take the tram.' It might even go so far – though even members of the Anthroposophical Society are unlikely to take things this far that people will not go on trains, and so on. This would be complete nonsense, of course. It is not a matter of avoiding things but of getting a clear picture, real insight into the iron necessities of human evolution. Civilization cannot continue in an unbroken upward trend; it has to go through a succession of rising and falling waves.

There is, however, something else which can happen, something people generally do not want to know about today but which is exactly what modern humanity will have to discover. Insight – a clear picture of the necessity which exists – is what will have to come to all human minds. It will necessarily mean that much will have to change in the frame of mind in which we consider the world. Human beings will need to live with inner impulses which they still prefer to ignore today, for these go against the good life they want. There are many such impulses. Let me give you just one example.

People today, especially if they want to be good people, wanting nothing for themselves but only to be selfless and desire the good of others, will of course seek to develop certain virtues. These, too, are iron necessities. Now, of course, there is nothing to be said against a desire for virtue, but the problem is that people are not merely desiring to be virtuous. It is quite a good thing to want to be virtuous, but these people want more. If one looks to the unconscious depths of the human soul one finds that in the present time people are not really much concerned to develop the actual virtues. It is much more important to them to be able to feel themselves to be virtuous, to give themselves up entirely to a state of mind where they can say: 'I am truly selfless, look at all the things I do to improve myself! I am perfect, I am kind, I am someone who does not believe in authority.' They will then, of course, eagerly follow all kinds of authorities. To feel really good in the consciousness of having one particular virtue or another is endlessly more important to people today than actually having that virtue. They want to feel they have the virtue rather than practise it.

As a result, certain secrets connected with the virtues remain hidden to them. They are secrets which people instinctively feel they do not want to know, especially if they are modern idealists who like to feel good in the way I have described. All kinds of ideals are represented by societies today. Programmes are made, and a society states its principles, which are to achieve one thing or another. The things people want to achieve in this way may indeed be very nice, but to find something nice in an abstract way is not enough. People must learn to think in terms of reality. Let us look at the aspect of reality when it comes to people having virtues. Perfection, benevolence, beautiful virtues, rights – it is nice to have them all in the outer social sphere. However, when people say 'It is our programme to achieve perfection in some particular way, benevolence in some particular direction, we aim to establish a specific right,' they usually consider this to be something absolute which can be brought to realization as such. 'Surely,' people will say, 'it must be a good thing to be more and more perfect?' And, 'What better ideal can there be but to have a programme that will make us more and more perfect?' But this is not in accord with the law of reality. It is right, and good, to be more and more perfect, or at least aim to be so, but when people are actually seeking to be perfect in a particular direction, this search for perfection will after a time change into what in reality is imperfection. A change occurs through which the desire for perfection becomes a weakness. Benevolence will after a time become prejudicial behaviour. And however good the right may be that you want to bring to realization, it will turn into a wrong in the course of time. The reality is that there are no absolutes in this world. You work towards something that is good, and the way of the world will turn it into something bad. We therefore must seek ever new ways, look for new forms over and over again. This is what really matters.

The swing of the pendulum governs all such human efforts. Nothing is more harmful than belief in absolute ideals, for they are at odds with the true course of world evolution.

A good way of demonstrating things – not to prove, but merely to illustrate – is to use certain ideas. And to some extent, ideas from the physical sciences can be used as symbols to illustrate non-physical ideas. Imagine we have a pendulum suspended here [drawing on the board]. Now you see, if you take the pendulum to this point, to one extreme, and then let go, it will go to this point to find its equilibrium. It follows this path. Why does it do so? Because it is subject to gravity, people say. It goes down, but once it has reached the lowest point it does not stop there. The downward movement has given it a certain inertia, which it uses to move to the other side. It then goes down again. It means that when the pendulum travels this distance, the downward movement gives it sufficient energy to swing to the other side. This provides an analogy that may be used to give a strong visual image of one thing or another. Thus we may say: a virtue – perfection, benevolence – goes in this direction, but then goes in the opposite direction. Perfection becomes weakness, benevolence, uncritical adoration, and right turns into wrong in the course of evolution.

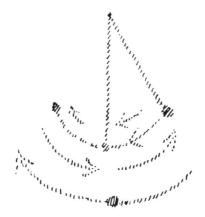

People prefer not to consider such ideas today. Just imagine trying to explain to a solid middle-class citizen who is establishing a society which is to serve certain ideals: 'You are now setting up an ideal, but in making it part of the process of evolution you will create the opposite effect, and you will do so in a relatively short time.' Well, he would think you are not only no idealist but a real devil. Why should the effort to be perfect not go towards increasing perfection, and why should right not continue to be right for ever and ever? It is extremely difficult for people today to have ideas based on reality instead of ideas that are one-sided abstractions. Yet they will have to learn to have such ideas, for they will not progress without them. They will also have to become used to the idea that progress in civilization will gradually make it necessary for us to use the elemental spirits of birth and death. And in doing so, humanity will have to live with the fact that a destructive element becomes part of human evolution.

Every now and then, people who refuse to familiarize themselves with anthroposophy – which is the only means of finding the right attitude to such things – find the right ideas by themselves, from instinct. What is the significance of all this? The elemental spirits of birth and death are, of course, messengers of Ahriman. The iron necessity of world evolution forces the gods to use Ahriman's messengers to control birth and death. When they ask the elemental spirits to act on their behalf they do not allow the powers of these messengers to enter the physical world. But as civilization goes into its decline, from the fifth post-Atlantean period onwards, this element has to come in again, so that catastrophe may be brought about. Human beings must use these powers themselves. Ahriman's messengers are therefore an iron necessity; they have to bring about the destruction that will lead to the next step forward in civilization. This is a terrible truth, but it is so. And nothing will avail where this truth is concerned but to get to know it and to see it clearly. We shall be discussing this further and you will see how many things there are which call for the right attitude to these truths.

Instinct, I have said, makes some people realize that something is necessary. One such individual is Ricarda Huch,[26] who has written a number of excellent books at the present time – though none that somehow comes even close to anthroposophy. Her latest work, on Luther's faith, is remarkable – not so much because of insight, but because of the instinct to be found in this book. If you read the first three chapters of the book you find there a strange cry – I think we may call it such – a cry for humanity to find again what has really been lost since Luther came on the scene. Before his day atavistic clairvoyance still existed. Ricarda Huch says that what humanity needs most of all today is to get to know the devil. She does not consider it so necessary for people to come

to know God; it is much more important, she says, to get to
know the devil.

Ricarda Huch does not know, of course, why this is necessary,
but she has an instinctive feeling that it is so. Hence her
remarkable cry for knowledge of the devil in the first chapters of
the book. This is highly symptomatic and significant for our
time. Her thinking is: people will come to know God again once
they know that the devil is all around them. Individuals like this,
who still do not want to take up anthroposophy, will always look
for a way to apologize for their statements. Ricarda Huch does
feel that people must get to know the devil as someone who is
very real; but she immediately says, as a kind of apology, that one
should not, of course, imagine the devil to be walking around in
the street with horns and a tail. Oh, but he does walk around!
'They never know the devil is about, not even when he has them
by the collar.'[27] Modern abstract thinking immediately needs an
apology, even if someone knows instinctively what is most
urgently needed. But there is a good and real instinct for the
present time behind this cry for the devil. People should not
simply grow blindly, as if asleep, into what iron necessity
demands of them in the immediate future, which is to use the
messengers of the devil in our work in laboratories, workshops,
banks and everywhere else. They have to use them so that
civilization may progress; but they must know the devil, they
must know that the keys which are used, say, to unlock the vaults
have the devil's power in them. Ricarda Huch knows this
instinctively, and people need to know it, for only knowledge will
take us into the future in the right way. It is of immense
importance that there are people who, out of instinct, point to
the need which exists to know the devil and not walk past him
fast asleep, for he is getting more and more powerful.

Perhaps there is something else that is characteristic – I
mention it only in passing: in Paradise, too, it was a woman who
instinctively allowed the functions of the devil to enter into
Paradise. I think it is not much to the credit of people in our
civilization that they are still calling this kind of thing superstition

and refuse to have anything to do with it, once again leaving it to a woman. It may indeed be characteristic that a woman, Ricarda Huch, is calling for the devil, just as once in Paradise it was Eve who let in the devil. This merely is a passing comment.

It is the devil who will and must be the bearer of our future civilization. This is a harsh truth, but it is important. It is intimately bound up with the fact that destructive powers will have to enter into the future progress of civilization. Above all, destructive powers will have to enter into the whole field of education, and especially the education of children, unless the matter is taken in hand with wisdom. Because of the general trend of civilization, and the customary practices and emotions of people, destructive powers will also enter more and more into the whole social sphere. They will, above all, bring more and more destruction into the actual relationships between people.

Humanity should seek to bring Christ's words to realization: 'Where two or three are gathered together in my name, there am I in the midst of them.'[28] Technological and commercial progress will not bring this to realization, but rather: Where two or more want to fight and assault each other in my name, there am I in the midst of them. This will happen more and more in the social life and because of this there is a general difficulty today in presenting truths which will bring people together.

Let us conclude by being clear in our minds, at least for the moment, about the frame of mind in which people generally receive truths. People do not like to be told truths today because they simply do not believe truth to be something which comes to human beings directly from the world of the spirit. Modern people believe truth must always be something grown in their own garden. People in their twenties have their own point of view, they do not need to be convinced of a truth, they do not need to have the truth revealed to them, they have their own point of view. And someone who has eagerly fought for the truth, a young fellow of 24, just finished at university where he may have attended lectures on philosophy – he has his point of view and enters into discussion with another who has just as eagerly fought for his own truth. Each of them believes that the absolute certain truth grows in his own garden, even if the soil has not been prepared. People are not inclined to receive truths; they announce themselves the possessors of truth. This is the characteristic element in the present time.

Ricarda Huch has put it rather nicely. She points out that in the period of Enlightenment in Europe our present state of mind, or call it what you will, which is absolutely awash with chauvinism, was preceded by Nietzscheanism, which was far more sublime than anything connected with native pride and chauvinism. Many, many people became followers of Nietzsche and it was he who set up the ideal of the 'tawny beast'. People actually had little idea of what this meant. Ricarda Huch says: People who did not even have what it takes to be a decent pet rabbit fancied themselves as 'tawny beasts' of the kind Nietzsche presented.[29] There you have the modern bourgeois point of view. One does not have what it takes to be a decent rabbit, but if someone establishes a high ideal – that is how they like to see themselves! One considers oneself to be this, without doing anything to achieve it. People do not feel they need to develop, for they cannot bear the idea of being something in the future; they want to be something now. This splits them apart into human atoms, each with his own point of view, with no one able to understand anyone else. There, in this mood where no one can understand anyone else, you see the destructive powers at work in human society. This is driving people apart. It was, of course, the devil who presented people with the temptation to be 'tawny beasts'. They did not actually become such beasts, but even so, the nineteenth-century impulses which destroy social life in the twentieth century have certainly taken root.

VII. Truth, Beauty, Goodness and the Elemental Beings

Dornach, 16 December 1922

THE FACULTIES needed by man in order that he may be able to confront the world and work in it during earthly life are connected, as I have shown, with his activities in the spiritual world between death and rebirth. This means, however, that here on earth man lives in certain spheres which on the earth itself have no inherent reality, which manifest their reality only when observed in the supersensible realm.[30]

We will turn our attention today to the three domains which actually comprise all human activity on earth: to the thoughts through which man endeavours to assimilate *Truth* in the world; to feelings, in so far as in and through his world of feeling, man endeavours to assimilate the *Beautiful;* to his will-nature, in so far as he is meant to bring the *Good* to fulfilment through it.

When we speak of thoughts, we mean that domain through which truth can be assimilated. But thoughts in themselves cannot be *real.* Precisely when we are clear that through our thoughts we have to inform ourselves about the truth of what is real, then it must also be admitted that thoughts, as such, cannot be anything real. Just imagine for a moment that you were to be fixed as firmly in your thoughts as you are in your brain or your heart; if that were the case, these thoughts would indeed be something real in themselves. We should not be able to assimilate reality through them. Nor could we ever express through human speech what human speech is intended to express if it contained full reality in the ordinary earthly sense. If every time we uttered a sentence we were obliged to work something heavy out of the mouth, we should be unable to *express* anything; it would rather be a matter of *producing* something. In this sense, what is spoken is not a reality in itself, but 'signifies' a reality, just as thoughts are not themselves a reality but merely signify a reality. And if we consider the good, then we shall find that what is formed through physical reality can never be called the good. We must bring up from the depths of our being the impulse to goodness, at first as something entirely unreal and then make it a reality. If the impulse to goodness were to arise like hunger, as an external reality, goodness is just what it could *not* be. Again, when you are looking at a statue it does not occur to you to think that you can converse with it. It is merely semblance; and in the semblance something is made manifest, namely, beauty. So that in *truth*, reality is certainly indicated. But truth itself moves in an element of unreality; and it is the same with *beauty*, the same with *goodness*.

It is therefore necessary for man that his thoughts are not, in themselves, real. Just imagine – if thoughts were to wander around in the head like leaden figures, then, to be sure, you would be aware of a reality, but these leaden thoughts would not be able to signify anything to you, they would be something real themselves. As truly as thoughts, as the beautiful and the good too cannot be directly real, so it is also true that reality is necessary in this physical-earthly world in order that we can have thoughts, make the beautiful manifest in the world through art, and also bring the good to fulfilment.

In speaking of this I come today to a domain of spiritual science which can lead us very deeply into the spirituality that is around us here on earth and is essential for earthly existence, but completely withdrawn from the observation possible to the senses and hence cannot be grasped by the ordinary consciousness which depends, as you know, entirely upon physical perception. The fact is that we are surrounded everywhere by spiritual beings of the greatest possible variety, only the ordinary consciousness does not perceive them. Their existence is necessary in order that as human beings we may be able to unfold our faculties, to have thoughts in their chimerical lightness and evanescence, so that they are not present in our heads like leaden weights, are not something real in themselves, but can 'signify' reality.

For this it is necessary that there should be beings in the world who prevent our thoughts with their non-reality from immediately vanishing from us again. We people are really too cumbersome, too ponderous, to be able without more ado to hold fast our thoughts with the ordinary consciousness. Elemental beings must be there, beings who help us ever and again to hold fast our thoughts. Such elemental beings are indeed present, only they are extraordinarily hard to discover because they always conceal themselves. When we ask: 'How does it really come about that we can hold fast a thought when it has no reality at all? Who is helping us to do this?' – even then it is very easy to be deceived, precisely when the matter is considered in the light of spiritual science. For at the very moment we begin to ask ourselves the question 'By whom are thoughts held fast for human beings?' – through this very desire to know about the spirit-entities who hold thoughts fast, we are driven into the realm of the ahrimanic beings. We plunge into the realm of these beings and very soon begin to believe – although it is of course a deceptive belief – that man must be supported by the ahrimanic spirits in order to hold fast the thoughts, so that they shall not vanish the moment he grasps them. On this account, most people are – unconsciously – even grateful to the ahrimanic beings for supporting them in their thinking. But it is misplaced gratitude, for there is a whole kingdom of beings who support us in our thought-world particularly, and who are by no means ahrimanic.

These beings are difficult to find in the spiritual world, even for well-trained vision. One finds them sometimes by observing a very clever person at work; if one watches such a person one can perceive that he actually has a volatile, fleeting band of followers. He does not go about alone but has a fugitive following of spiritual beings who do not belong to the ahrimanic kingdom, but who have an altogether remarkable character. One first really learns to know these beings when one can observe those *other* beings who belong to the ahrimanic realm, to the elemental kingdoms, and therefore are not perceptible to the eyes of the senses, who are at work when forms in nature, crystal forms, for example, arise. The activity of these beings underlies all form; you find them described in my Mystery Plays as beings who chisel and hammer out solid forms. If you think of the gnome-like beings in one of the Mystery Plays[31] you have there the beings who produce forms. Now these beings are sly and crafty – as you can see from the way I have presented them in the play – and they mock at the scanty intelligence possessed by people. Call to mind those scenes from the Mystery Play if they are known to you.

Now if we observe a really clever person and perceive how he may have a retinue consisting of a whole host of such beings as I have described, we find that these beings are despised by the gnome-spirits of the elemental world because they are clumsy and, above all, because they are terribly foolish. Foolishness is their main characteristic! And so it can be said that precisely the very cleverest people in the world, when we can observe them from this aspect, are followed by whole troops of 'spirit-fools'. It is as if these foolish spirits wanted to belong to someone. And they are greatly disdained by the beings who fashion and shape forms in nature in the way described in the Mystery Plays. We can therefore say: among the worlds unknown, to begin with, to ordinary consciousness, there is one that is peopled by a spirit-folk of 'fools', fools who throng towards human wisdom and cleverness. In the present age these beings have actually no life of their own. They achieve a life by using the life of those who are dying, who are dying from illness but in whom life-forces are still present. These beings can only make use of a life that is past. Thus there are spirit-fools who use the life that remains over from human beings; they sate themselves with the life that lingers in cemeteries and such places.

It is when we penetrate into worlds like this that we realize how densely populated is the realm lying behind the world that is perceptible to the senses, how manifold are the classes of spirit-beings, and how closely connected these spirit-beings are with our faculties. A clever person pursuing his activities, who is merely clever and not clairvoyant, can hold fast his thoughts precisely through the fact that he is followed by this troop of spirit-fools. These spirit-fools rivet themselves to his thoughts, drag at them and give them weight, so that they remain with him, whereas otherwise they would quickly vanish from him.

These beings are, as I said, bitterly scoffed at by the gnome-like beings. The gnome-like beings will not tolerate them in their realm although they belong to it. The gnome-like beings drive the others away continually and there is a hard fight between the gnome-folk and this folk of spirit-fools through whom alone wisdom is made possible for man; otherwise the wisdom would be fugitive, would pass away the moment it came into existence, could not remain. As has been said, these beings are hard to discover because it is so easy to fall into the ahrimanic sphere directly questions are asked about them. But one can find them on occasions such as I have just indicated, by observing very clever people who are followed by a whole troop of such beings. Apart from that, however, when there are not enough clever thoughts fastening on to people, these beings are to be found lingering, for example, in libraries – when the books contain clever material. When the contents of books are stupid these beings are not to be found; they are to be found only where there is cleverness. On that they rivet themselves.

This gives us some insight into a realm that surrounds us everywhere, that is present just as the nature-kingdoms are present, that has something to do with our faculties, but is very difficult to assess. If we wish to do that we must rely upon those gnome-like beings and set some store by their judgement – and they, in fact, consider the other beings stupid and impudent.

But these other beings have yet another characteristic.

When they are too severely persecuted by the gnome-like beings, they escape into human heads, and whereas outside in nature they are almost giants – of an enormous size – they become quite tiny when they are inside people's heads. One could say that they are an abnormal species of nature-spirits, who are, however, intimately connected with the whole of human evolution on the earth.

Beings of another kind live chiefly in the watery and airy elements, just as do those beings described in the Mystery Plays as the sylph-like beings. The beings to whom I am now referring have chiefly to do with the world of 'beautiful semblance'. They attach themselves less to people who are clever in the ordinary sense than to those who are genuinely artistic in nature. But these beings too are very hard to discover as they can so easily conceal themselves. They are to be found where there are genuine works of art, where, for instance, the human form or forms of nature and so forth are portrayed in semblance. There they are to be found.

These beings too, as I said, can only be discovered with difficulty. When, for instance, we ask how it is that beautiful semblance interests us, that there are occasions when we derive greater pleasure from a beautiful statue than from a living person (true, it is a different kind of pleasure, but for all that, greater), or that we are edified and delighted by melodies or harmonies? – when we ask ourselves this we very easily fall into a different realm, into the realm of the luciferic beings. It is not only the luciferic beings who promote enthusiasm for art, but again there is a kingdom of elemental beings by whom interest in art is stimulated and kept alive in man. Without such beings man would never be disposed to take an interest in beautiful semblance, simply because it is unreal.

Now the reason why it is so difficult to discover these beings is because they can conceal themselves even more easily than the spirit-fools, for they are actually only present where beauty makes its power felt. And when we are wrapt in enjoyment of the beautiful, then we certainly do not see these beings. Why is this?

In order to get a sight of them in a normal way we must endeavour, while given up in some way to artistic impressions, to direct clairvoyant vision to the beings who are depicted in the same scene in the Mystery Play as nymph- or sylph-like beings; these beings too belong to the elemental nature-kingdoms, and we must project ourselves into them. We must, as it were, look *with* these air- and water-beings at the others who are present whenever joy is taken in beauty. And as this is difficult we must turn to other means of help. Now fortunately it is easy to discover these beings when we are listening to someone who speaks beautifully and whose language we do not properly understand, when we hear only the sounds without understanding the meaning. If we then abandon ourselves to the experience of this beautiful speaking – but it must be *really* beautiful speaking, genuine oratory, and we must not be able to understand it properly – then we can acquire the faculty, intimate and delicate as it is, of seeing these beings.

Thus we must try, as it were, to acquire the talent of the sylphs and to strengthen it through what unfolds when we listen to beautiful speech without endeavouring to understand the meaning but having ears only for its beauty. Then we discover the beings who are present wherever beauty is and who lend their support so that man can have a true interest in it.

And then follows the disillusionment, the great and terrible surprise. For these beings are in fact hideously ugly, the very ugliest that can be imagined; they are ghastly creatures, the very archetypes of ugliness. And if we have developed the requisite spiritual vision and visit some studio where artistic work is being done, we find that it is these beings who are present on earth, like spiders on the ground of world-existence, in order that people may take interest in beauty. It is through these frightful spider-creatures of an elemental order that interest in beauty really awakens. Man simply could not have the right interest in beauty if in his life of soul he were not entangled in a world of hideously ugly spider-like beings.

When they are going through a gallery, people have no

inkling – for what I have said refers only to discovering the *form* of these beings, who are always present when anyone is delighting in beauty – people have no inkling of how they are strengthened in the interest they take in beautiful pictures by having these hideous spider-like creatures creeping in and out of their ears and nostrils.

Man's enthusiasm for what is beautiful arises on the foundation of ugliness. That is a cosmic secret, my dear friends. The spur of ugliness is needed in order that the beautiful may be made manifest. And the greatest artists were people who because of their strong bodily constitution could endure the invasions of these spidery beings in order to produce, let us say, a *Sistine Madonna*, or the like. Whatever beauty is brought forth in the world has been lifted out of a sea of ugliness through the enthusiasm in the human soul.

Let it not be thought that behind the veil of the material world, in the region beyond the threshold, we come into a realm of pure beauty. Do not imagine that anyone who is cognizant of these things speaks lightheartedly when he says that if people are not properly prepared they must be held back at the threshold of the spiritual world. For it is essential first of all to know the thoroughly unedifying foundations of all that, in front of the curtain as it were, is uplifting and edifying.

Therefore if with spiritual sight we move about the elemental world belonging to air and water, again we see the great battle waging between the fleeting sylphs and undines and these archetypes of ugliness. Although I spoke of the latter as spidery creatures, the tissues of which they are formed are not like those of spiders as we know them, but they are composed of the elements of water and watery vapour. They are volatile air-formations, the ugliness of which is enhanced inasmuch as every second they have a different ugliness; each succeeding ugliness gives the impression of being even worse than its predecessor. This world is present in air and water together with everything that is delightful there.

And now in order that man may unfold enthusiasm for the good something else takes place. It can be said of the other beings that they are more or less actually there, but in the case of the beings of whom I am now going to speak it must really be said that they are continually coming into existence, whenever, in fact, a person has within him warmth of feeling for goodness. It is in this warmth that these beings develop; their nature itself is warm and fiery; they live in the present but their inherent nature is similar to what I have described in the book *Occult Science* in connection with the Saturn-existence of man.

As man was in the Old Saturn-existence, so are these beings today. Their form is not the same but their nature is similar. It cannot be said of them that they are beautiful or ugly, or anything of that kind; they must be judged in comparison with the ordinary elemental warmth-beings who, as you know, also exist. All spiritual research in this sphere is extraordinarily difficult. It is very difficult to approach the beings who live entirely in warmth, that is to say, in 'fire' in the old sense, and when one does come upon them it is not very pleasant. One comes upon them, for instance, when lying in a high fever, but then as a rule one is not a really objective observer. Otherwise it is a matter of developing the requisite faculty for perceiving these warmth-beings by elaborating the methods indicated in my books. These warmth-beings have a certain relationship with the beings who appear, for instance, when a person has warm enthusiasm for the good, but the relationship is of a very peculiar kind. I will assume hypothetically – for only in that way can I describe these things – that warmth-beings of the normal kind are present, originating in man's physical warmth, which as you know is greater than the warmth of the environment. Man has his own warmth, hence these particular beings are near him. And now, in a person who has enthusiasm for the good these *other* beings make themselves manifest; they too are warmth-beings, but of a different kind. When they are in the neighbourhood of the normal fire-beings they immediately draw back from them and slip into the inmost recesses of man's nature. If one then makes great efforts to discover their essential characteristics in contrast to those of the normal warmth-beings, one finds that they have an inner, but very pronounced, bashfulness. They refuse absolutely to be observed by other beings of the spiritual world, and flee from them because they are ashamed of being seen; they flee first and foremost into the inmost nature of man. Hence they are hard to discover. Actually they are only to be discovered if we observe ourselves in certain moments that it is really not so very easy to bring about at will. Just suppose that in spite of not being in the least sentimental we are moved to tears simply by reading a scene in a book that grips us deeply and dramatically. Some great and good action is described, let us say, in a novel. If we have the power of self-observation we can discover how whole hosts of such beings (who have such delicate sensibility that they do not want to be seen by any other beings of the spiritual world) flee into our heart, into our breast, how they come to us, how they seek protection from the other warmth-beings and in fact from any other beings of the elemental spiritual worlds.

There is a significant force of repulsion between the normal warmth-beings and these other warmth beings with their intense bashfulness who live only in the sphere of man's moral life and who flee from contact with other spirit-beings. These beings are present in far greater numbers than is usually imagined and it is they who imbue man with enthusiasm for the morally good. Man would not readily acquire this enthusiasm for the morally good if these beings did not come to his aid; and when a person loves the moral, he has a real bond, an unconscious bond, with these beings.

Certain of their characteristics are such as may lead us to misunderstand this whole kingdom. For after all, why do these beings feel bashful and ashamed? It is actually because all the other beings in the elemental kingdoms of the spiritual world in which they live disdain them, will have nothing to do with them. They are aware of this and the disdain to which they are subjected causes them to stimulate enthusiasm for the good.

These beings have certain other characteristics of which I

do not care to speak, for the human soul is so obviously upset at any mention of such hideous spidery creatures. I therefore prefer not to refer to certain of their peculiarities. But at any rate we have heard how what unfolds in the realm of the senses as the true, the beautiful, the good, unfolds from foundations which need the three spiritual kingdoms I have described, just as we on earth need the ground on which we walk. These beings do not create the true, the beautiful or the good. But the thoughts which express the true, and signify the true, need the spirit-dunderheads, so that they may move on their shoulders. The beautiful that man produces needs the ugly water- and air-spiders so that it can raise itself out of this ocean of ugliness. And the good needs a kingdom of beings who cannot show themselves at all among the other normal warmth-beings, who must always fight shy of them, and for this very reason evoke enthusiasm for the good.

If these beings did not exist, then instead of thoughts in our heads we should have, if not exactly leaden soldiers, at least heavy vapours, and nothing clever could possibly result. In order to produce the beautiful we should need to have the gift of imbuing it with actual life in order that people's interest might be aroused. In order that here, in the world of the senses, there may be at hand what we need for the activity of thought, for the sense of beauty, for the will to arouse enthusiasm for the good – for this, three such elemental kingdoms are necessary.

The normal elemental kingdoms – that is, the kingdoms of the gnomes, sylphs, undines and salamanders, to use folk-terminology – are still at the stage of striving to become something in the world. They are on the way to having forms resembling those in our sense-world; the forms will not be the same, but one day they will become perceptible to the senses possessed by people today, whereas now, in their elementary existence, these beings are not perceptible to the ordinary senses.

The beings I have now described to you have in fact already by-passed the stage at which human beings and animals and plants are today. So that if, for example, we were able to go back to the Old Moon-existence which preceded the earth, we should there encounter the beings found on earth today as the bashful beings connected with moral impulses in man. On the Old Moon they would have been perceptible as a real animal world, spinning as it were from tree to tree. But you must call to mind the Old Moon-existence as I have described it in the book *Occult Science*. Everything in this Moon-existence was pliable and fluid and metamorphosis has continually taken place. Among the beings there, spinning in and out, were those hideous beings I have described, those spidery creatures permeating the Old Moon and visible there. And there were also present the beings who as spirit-fools accompany the wise on the earth today. They were a factor in bringing about the destruction of the Old Moon, so that the earth could arise. And even now, during earth-existence, these beings have no pleasure in the formation of crystals, but rather in the breaking up of everything mineral.

Thus while we can say of the normal elemental beings that they will one day become visible to the senses, we must say of these other beings: once upon a time they were visible to the senses and have now sprung over into the spiritual – admittedly through their luciferic and ahrimanic natures. Thus there are two kinds of elemental beings – ascending and descending. We can say: on the 'dung' of Old Moon ugliness – which was there in profusion during the Old Moon-existence – on the 'dung' of Old Moon ugliness, our world of beauty springs forth.

You have an analogy in nature when you carry manure to the fields and beautiful plants spring from it. There you have an analogy in nature except that the dung, the manure, is also perceptible to the senses. So it is when the half-reality of the world of beauty is observed clairvoyantly. Try to envisage this half-real world of beauty, quite apart from the teeming life in the three kingdoms of nature on the earth; picture all the beautiful after-effects springing from the earth. Just as lovely flowers spring up in a meadow, you must spiritually picture underneath it all the Moon-dung which contains the ugly spidery creatures

I have described. Just as cabbage does not grow unless it is manured, as little can beauty blossom on the earth unless the gods manure the earth with ugliness. That is the inner necessity of life. And this inner necessity of life must be known to us, for such knowledge alone can give us the power to confront with understanding what actually surrounds us in nature.

Anyone who believes that beauty in art can be produced on earth without the foundation of this ugliness is like a person who is horrified that people use manure, insisting that it would be far better to let beautiful things grow without it. In point of fact it is not possible for beauty to be produced without the foundation of ugliness. And if people do not want to give themselves up to illusion about the world, that is, if they genuinely desire to know the essential and not the illusory, then they must acquire knowledge of these things. Whoever believes that there is art in the world without ugliness does not know what art is. And why not? Simply for the reason that only he who has an inkling of what I have described to you today will enjoy works of art in the right way, for he knows at what cost they are purchased in world-existence. Whoever wants to enjoy works of art without this consciousness is like a person who would prefer to do away with manure on the fields. Such a person has no real knowledge of what grows in nature; he has, in fact, merely an illusion before him – plants of papier mâché, although real plants are actually there. Whoever does not feel ugliness as the foundation has not the right kind of delight in beauty.

Such is the world-order, and people must acquire knowledge of it if they do not want to go on wandering about like earthworms, keeping to their own element and not looking upwards to what is real. People can only develop the talents latent within them if they confront reality fairly and squarely. Reality, however, is not attained merely by talking time and time again of spirit, spirit, spirit, but by really coming to know the spiritual. But the fact has also to be faced that in certain regions of the spiritual world something like I have been describing to you today will be encountered.

VIII. Elemental Spirits and the Plant World

Dornach, 2 November 1923

To the outwardly perceptible, visible world there belongs the invisible world, and these, taken together, form a whole. The marked degree to which this is the case first appears in its full clarity when we turn our attention away from the animals to the plants.

Plant life, as it sprouts and springs forth from the earth, immediately arouses our delight, but it also provides access to something which we must feel to be full of mystery. In the case of the animal, though certainly its will and whole inner activity have something of the mysterious, we nevertheless recognize that this will is actually there, and is the cause of the animal's form and outer characteristics. But in the case of the plants, which appear on the face of the earth in such magnificent variety of form, which develop in such a mysterious way out of the seed with the help of earth and the surrounding air – in the case of the plant we feel that some other factor must be present in order that this plant world may arise in the form it does.

When spiritual vision is directed to the plant world, we are immediately led to a whole host of beings which were known and recognized in the old times of instinctive clairvoyance but which were afterwards forgotten, and today remain only as names used by the poet, names to which modern man ascribes no reality. To the same degree, however, in which we deny reality to the beings that flit so busily around the plants, to that degree do we lose the understanding of the plant world. This understanding of the plant world, which, for instance, would be so necessary for the practice of medicine, has been entirely lost to present-day humanity.

We have already recognized a very significant connection

between the world of plants and the world of butterflies; but this too will only really come alive for us when we look yet more deeply into the whole range of activities and processes that go on in the plant world.

Plants send down their roots into the ground. Anyone who can observe what they really send down and can perceive the roots with spiritual vision (for this he must have) sees how the root is everywhere surrounded by the activities of elemental nature spirits. And these elemental spirits, which an old clairvoyant perception designated as gnomes and which we may call the root spirits, can actually be studied with Imagination and Inspiration,[32] just as human life and animal life can be studied in the physical world. We can look into the soul nature of these elemental spirits, into this world of the spirits of the roots.

The root spirits are quite special earth folk, invisible at first to outer view but in their effects so much the more visible; for no root could develop if it were not for what is mediated between the root and the earth realm by these remarkable root spirits, which bring the mineral element of the earth into flux in order to conduct it to the roots of plants. I am of course referring to the underlying spiritual process.

These root spirits, which are everywhere present in the earth, get a quite particular sense of well-being from rocks and from ores (which may be more or less transparent and also contain metallic elements). They have the greatest feeling of well-being in this sphere because it is the place where they belong, where they are conveying what is mineral to the roots of the plants. And they are filled with an inner spirituality that we can only compare with the inner spirituality of the human eye and the human ear. For these root spirits are in their spiritual nature entirely sense. Apart from this they are nothing at all; they consist only of sense. They are entirely sense, and it is a sense which is at the same time *intellect*, which does not only see and hear but immediately understands what is seen and heard; it not only receives impressions, but everywhere also receives ideas.

We can even indicate the way in which these root spirits receive their ideas. We see a plant sprouting out of the earth. The plant comes, as I shall presently show, in connection with the extra-terrestrial universe; and, particularly at certain seasons of the year, spiritual currents flow from above, from the flower and the fruit of the plant down into the root, streaming into the earth. And just as we turn our eyes towards the light and see, so do the root spirits turn their faculty of perception towards what trickles downwards from above, through the plant into the earth. What trickles down towards the root spirits is something which the light has sent into the flowers, which the heat of the sun has sent into the plants, which the air has produced in the leaves, which the distant stars have brought about in creating the plant form. The plant gathers the secrets of the universe, sends them into the ground, and the gnomes take these secrets into themselves from what trickles down spiritually to them through the plants. And because the gnomes, particularly from autumn on and through the winter, in their wanderings through ore and rock, bear with them what has trickled down to them through the plants, they are the beings within the earth which carry the ideas of the whole universe as they stream and wander through the earth.

We look out into the wide world. The world has been built in the spirit of the universe; it is an embodiment of the ideas of the universe, of the spirit of the universe. Through the plants, which to them are the same as rays of light are to us, the gnomes take in the ideas of the universe and carry them in full consciousness from metal to metal, from rock to rock within the earth.

We gaze down into the depths of the earth, not to seek there below for abstract ideas about some kind of mechanical laws of nature but to behold the roving, wandering gnomes, which are the light-filled preservers of the world intellect within the earth.

These gnomes have immediate understanding of what they see; their knowledge is of a similar nature to that of man, but theirs is the intellect of intellects, and they are nothing but intellect. Everything about them is intellect, an intellect so universal that they look down on the human intellect as something imperfect. The gnomes laugh us to scorn on account of the groping, struggling intellect with which we manage to grasp one thing or another, whereas they have no need at all to think things out. They have direct perception of what is sensible and intelligent in the world; and they are particularly ironical when they notice the efforts people have to make to come to this or that conclusion. Why should they do this? say the gnomes – why ever should people give themselves so much trouble to think things over? We know everything we look at. People are so stupid – say the gnomes – for they must first think things over.

And I must say that gnomes can be ironical to the point of ill manners if one speaks to them of logic. For why ever should people need such a superfluous thing – a training in thinking? The thoughts are already there. The ideas flow through the plants. Why don't people stick their noses into the earth down to the depth of the plant's roots, and let what the sun says to the plants trickle down into their noses? Then they would know something! But with logic – say the gnomes – one can only have odd bits and pieces of knowledge.

Thus the gnomes are actually the bearers of the ideas of the universe, of the cosmos, inside the earth. But for the earth itself they have no liking at all. They flit about in the earth with ideas of the universe, but they actually hate what is earthly. This is something from which the gnomes would best like to escape. Nevertheless they remain with the earthly – you will soon see why this is so – but they hate it, for the earthly threatens them with a continual danger. The earth continually holds over them the threat of forcing them to take on particular shapes, the configuration of the creatures such as the amphibians, and in particular of frogs and toads. The feeling of the gnomes within the earth is really this: if we grow too strongly together with the earth, we shall assume the form of frogs or toads. They are continually on the alert to avoid being caught up too strongly in the earth and be forced to take on such an earthly form. They are always on the defensive against this earthly form, which threatens them in the element in which they exist in the way I have described. They have their home in the element of earth and moisture; there they live under the constant threat of being forced into amphibian forms. From this they continually tear themselves free by filling themselves entirely with the ideas of the extra-terrestrial universe. The gnomes are really the element within the earth which represents the extra-terrestrial, because they must continually avoid growing together with the earthly; otherwise they would individually take on the forms of the amphibian world. And it is just from what I may call this feeling of hatred, this feeling of antipathy towards the earthly, that the gnomes gain the power of driving the plants up from the earth. With the fundamental force of their being they unceasingly thrust away from the earthly, and it is this thrust that determines the upward direction of plant growth; they forcefully take the plants along with them. The antipathy that the gnomes have to anything earthly causes the plant to have only its roots in the earth and then grow out of the earth; in fact, the gnomes force the plants out of their true, original form and make them grow upwards and out of the earth.

Once the plant has grown upwards, once it has left the domain of the gnomes and has passed out of the sphere of the element of moist earth into the sphere of moist air, the plant develops what comes to outer physical form in the leaves. Other beings are at work now in everything that goes on in the leaves – water spirits, elemental spirits of the watery element, to which an earlier instinctive clairvoyance gave among others the name of undines. Where we found gnome beings flitting busily around the roots, we see close to the soil these water beings, these elemental beings of the water, these undines, observing with pleasure the upward-striving growth that the gnomes have produced.

These undine beings differ in their inner nature from the gnomes. They cannot turn outwards towards the universe like a spiritual sense organ. They can only yield themselves up to the movement and activity of the whole cosmos in the element of air and moisture, and they therefore do not have the clarity of mind that the gnomes have. They dream incessantly, these undines, but their dream is at the same time their own form. They do not hate the earth as intensely as do the gnomes, but they have a sensitivity to what is earthly. They live in the etheric element of water, swimming and floating in it. They are highly sensitive to anything in the nature of a fish; for the fish's form is a threat to them. They do assume it from time to time, though only to forsake it immediately in order to take on another metamorphosis. They dream their own existence. And in dreaming their own existence they bind and release, they bind and separate the substances of the air, which in a mysterious way they introduce into the leaves. They take these substances to the plants that the gnomes have thrust upwards. The plants would wither at this point if it were not for the undines, who approach from all sides. And as they move around the plants in their dreamlike consciousness, they prove to be what we can only call the world chemists. The undines dream the binding and releasing of substances. And this dream, in which the plant has its existence, into which it grows when, developing upwards, it leaves the ground, this undine dream is the world chemist which brings about the mysterious combining and separation of substances in the plant world, starting in the leaf. We can therefore say that the undines are the chemists of plant life. They dream of chemistry. They possess an exceptionally delicate spirituality which is really in its element just where water and air come in contact with each other. The undines live entirely in the element of moisture, but they feel their own inner satisfaction when they come to the surface of something watery, be it only a drop of water or something else of a watery nature. For their whole endeavour lies in preserving themselves from totally assuming the form of a fish, the permanent form of a fish. They wish to remain in a state of metamorphosis, in a state of eternal, endlessly continuing changeability. But in this state of changeability, in which they dream of the stars and of the sun, of light and of heat, they become the chemists who now, starting from the leaf, continue with the further development of the plant form that has been thrust upwards by the gnomes. So the plant develops its leaf growth, and this mystery is now revealed as the dream of the undines into which the plants grow.

To the same degree, however, in which the plant grows into the dream of the undines, it now enters into another domain higher up, into the domain of the spirits which live in the element of air and warmth, just as the gnomes live in that of earth and moisture and the undines in the element of air and moisture. In the element of air and warmth live the beings which an earlier clairvoyant faculty designated as the sylphs. Because air is everywhere imbued with light, these sylphs, which live in the element of air and warmth, press towards the light and become related to it. They are particularly susceptible to the finer but larger movements within the atmosphere.

When in spring or autumn you see a flock of swallows, which produce vibrations in a body of air as they fly along, creating a current of air, this moving air current – and this holds good for every bird – is something the sylphs can hear. Cosmic music is what they hear from it. If, let us say, you are travelling somewhere by ship and the seagulls are flying towards it, their flight sets in motion spiritual sounds, a spiritual music that accompanies the ship.

Again it is the sylphs which unfold and develop their being within this sounding music, finding themselves at home in the moving current of air. It is in this spiritually sounding, moving element of air that they find themselves at home; and at the same time they absorb what the power of light sends into these vibrations of the air. Because of this the sylphs, which experience existence more or less in a state of sleep, feel most in their element, most at home, where birds are winging through the air. If a sylph is obliged to flit through air devoid of birds, it feels as

though it had lost itself. But at the sight of a bird in the air
something quite special comes over the sylph. I have often had
to describe a certain event in human life, the event which leads
the human soul to address itself as 'I'. And I have always drawn
attention to the statement made by the French writer Jean Paul
that when for the first time a human being arrives at the
conception of his 'I' it is as though he looks into the most deeply
veiled Holy of Holies of his soul.[33] A sylph does not look into any
such a veiled Holy of Holies of its own soul, but when it sees a
bird a feeling of ego comes over it. It is in what the bird sets in
motion as it flies through the air that the sylph feels its ego. And
because this is so, because its ego is kindled in it from outside,
the sylph becomes the bearer of cosmic love through the
atmosphere. It is because the sylph embodies something like a
human wish, but does not have its ego within itself but in the bird
kingdom, that it is at the same time the bearer of wishes of love
through the universe.

Thus we behold the deepest sympathy between the sylphs
and the bird world. The gnome hates the amphibian world,
the undine is sensitive to fishes, is unwilling to approach
them, seeks to avoid them and feels a kind of horror for them.
The sylph, on the other hand, is attracted towards birds, and
has a sense of well-being when it can waft towards their
plumage, the floating air filled with sound. And were you to
ask a bird from whom it learns to sing, you would hear that its
inspirer is the sylph. Sylphs feel a sense of pleasure in the
bird's form. They are, however, prevented by the cosmic
ordering from becoming birds, for they have another task.
Their task is lovingly to convey light to the plant. And just as
the undine is the chemist for the plant, so is the sylph the light
bearer. The sylph imbues the plant with light; it bears light
into the plant.

Through the fact that the sylphs bear light into the plant,
something quite remarkable is brought about. You see, the
sylph is continually carrying light into the plant. The light,
that is to say the power of the sylphs in the plant, works on the

chemical forces that were induced into the plant by the undines. Here occurs the interworking of the sylph's light and the undine's chemistry. This is a remarkable moulding and shaping activity. With the help of the upstreaming substances which are worked on by the undines, the sylphs weave an ideal plant form out of the light. They actually weave the archetypal plant within the plant from light and from the chemical working of the undines. And when towards autumn the plant withers and everything of physical substance disperses, then the forms of the plants begin to trickle downwards, and now the gnomes perceive them, perceive what the world – the sun through the sylphs, the air through the undines – has brought to pass in the plant. This the gnomes perceive, and throughout the entire winter they are engaged in perceiving below what has trickled down into the soil from the plants. Down there they grasp world ideas in the plant forms which have been given shape and form with the help of the sylphs, and which now enter into the soil in their spiritual ideal form.

People who regard the plant as something material will of course know nothing of this spiritual ideal form.[34] Thus at this point a colossal error, a terrible error appears in the materialistic observation of the plant. I will give you a brief outline of this.

Everywhere you will find that in materialistic science matters are described as follows. The plant takes root in the ground, above the ground it develops its leaves and finally its flowers and within the flower the stamens, then the carpel.[35] The pollen from the anthers – usually from another plant – is taken over to the stigma, the carpel is fertilized and through this the seed of the new plant is produced. That is the usual way of describing it. The carpel is regarded as the female element and what comes from the stamens as the male – indeed matters cannot be regarded otherwise as long as people remain fixed in materialism, for then this process really does look like fertilization. This, however, it is not. In order to gain insight into the process of fertilization, that is to say the process of reproduction, in the plant world, we must be conscious that in the first place the plant form arises through the work of those great chemists, the undines, and the work of the sylphs. This is the ideal plant form which goes down into the ground and is taken care of by the gnomes. It is there below, this plant form. And there within the earth it is now guarded by the gnomes after they have seen and perceived it. The earth becomes the womb for what thus trickles downwards. This is something quite different from what is described in materialistic science.

After it has passed through the sphere of the sylphs, the plant comes into the sphere of the elemental fire spirits. These are the inhabitants of the element of heat and light. When the warmth of the earth is at its height, or otherwise at the right level, it is gathered up by the fire spirits. Just as the sylphs gather up the light, so do the fire spirits gather up the warmth and carry it into the flowers of the plant.

Undines carry the action of the chemical ether into the plants, sylphs the action of the light ether into the flowers, and the pollen provides what may be called little airships that enable the fire spirits to carry the warmth into the seed. Everywhere warmth is collected with the help of the stamens, and is carried by means of the pollen from the anthers to the seeds in the carpel. And what is formed here in the carpel in its entirety is the male element that comes from the cosmos. It is not a case of the carpel being female and the anthers of the stamens being male. In no way does fertilization occur in the flowers but only the preforming of the male seed. Fertilization occurs when the cosmic male seed taken from the warmth of the universe in the flower by the fire spirits is brought together with the female principle that has trickled down into the soil as an ideal element at an earlier stage, as I have described, and is resting there.

For plants the earth is the mother, the heavens the father. And all that takes place outside the domain of the earth is not the maternal womb for the plant. It is a colossal error to believe that the maternal principle of the plant is in the carpel. This

Male

Fire Spirits

Red

is in fact the male principle which has been drawn forth from the universe with the aid of the fire spirits. The maternal element is taken from the cambium of the plant, which lies between bark and wood, and carried down as ideal form. And what now results from the combined gnomes' and fire spirits' activity – this is fertilization. The gnomes are, in fact, the spiritual midwives of plant reproduction. Fertilization takes place below in the earth during the winter, when the seed comes into the earth and meets with the forms which the gnomes have received from the activities of the sylphs and undines and now carry to where these forms can meet with the fertilizing seeds.

You see, because people do not recognize what is spiritual, do not know that gnomes, undines, sylphs and fire spirits – which were formerly called salamanders – are actively involved in plant growth, there is a complete lack of clarity about the process of fertilization in the plant world. Up there, outside the earth, nothing by way of fertilization takes place; the earth is the mother of the plant world, the heavens the father. This is the case in a quite literal sense. Plant fertilization takes place through the fact that the gnomes take from the fire spirits what the fire spirits have carried into the carpel as concentrated cosmic warmth on the little airships of the anther pollen. Thus the fire spirits are the bearers of warmth.

And now you will easily gain insight into the whole process of plant growth. First, with the help of what comes from the fire spirits, the gnomes down below instil life into the plant and push it upwards. They are the fosterers of life. They carry the life ether to the root – the same life ether in which they themselves live. The undines foster the chemical ether in the plant, the sylphs the light ether, the fire spirits the warmth ether. And then the fruit of the warmth ether again unites with what is present below as life. Thus plants can only be understood when they are considered in connection with all that is flitting around them full of life and activity. And one only reaches the right interpretation of the most important process in the plant when one penetrates into these things in a spiritual way.

When once this has been understood, it is interesting to look again at the words Goethe jotted down when, in connection with another botanist, he was terribly annoyed because people speak of the eternal marriages going on up there in the plants.[36] Goethe was affronted by the idea that endless marriages should be consummated all over every meadow. This seemed to him something unnatural. In this Goethe had an instinctive but very true feeling. He could not as yet know the real facts of the matter, but nevertheless his instinct was a sure one. He could not see why fertilization should take place up there in the flower. He did not as yet know what goes on below ground and that the earth is the maternal womb of the plants. But he instinctively knew that the process which takes place in the flower is not what all botanists take it to be.[37]

You are now aware of the inner connection between plant and earth. But there is something else which you must take into account.

You see, when up above the fire spirits are flitting around the plant and transmitting the pollen from the anthers, they have only one feeling, which they have in an enhanced degree compared to the feeling of the sylphs. The sylphs experience their self, their ego, when they see the birds flit about. The fire spirits have this experience, but to an intensified degree, in regard to the butterfly world and indeed the insect world as a whole. And it is these fire spirits which take the utmost delight in following in the tracks of the insects' flight so that they convey warmth to the carpel. In order to carry the concentrated warmth, which must descend into the earth so that it may be united with the ideal form, the fire spirits feel themselves intimately related to the butterfly world and to the world of the insects in general. Everywhere they follow in the tracks of the insects as they flit from flower to flower. And so one really has the feeling, when following the flight of insects, that each of these insects as it flits from flower to flower has a quite special aura which cannot be entirely explained from the insect itself. Particularly the luminous, wonderfully radiant, shimmering aura of bees as they flit from flower to flower is unusually difficult to explain. And why? It is because the bee is everywhere accompanied by a fire spirit which feels so closely related to it that, for spiritual vision, the bee is surrounded by an aura which is actually a fire spirit. When a bee flies through the air from plant to plant, from tree to tree, it flies with an aura that is actually given to it by a fire spirit. The fire spirit does not only gain a feeling of its ego in the presence of the insect, but it wishes to be completely united with the insect.

Through this, insects also obtain that power about which I have spoken to you, and which shows itself in a shimmering forth of light into the cosmos. They obtain the power completely to spiritualize the physical matter which unites itself with them, and to allow the spiritualized physical substance to ray out into cosmic space. But just as with a flame it is heat in the first place which causes the light to shine, so, above the surface of the earth, when the insects shimmer forth into cosmic space and attract the human being to descend again into physical incarnation, it is the fire spirits which inspire the insects to this activity, the fire spirits that flit around them. But if the fire spirits are active in promoting the outstreaming of spiritualized matter into the cosmos, they are no less actively engaged in seeing to it that the concentrated fiery element, the concentrated warmth, goes into the interior of the earth, so that, with the help of the gnomes, the spirit form, which sylphs and undines cause to trickle down into the earth, may be awakened.

This, you see, is the spiritual process of plant growth. And it is because the subconscious in man divines something of a special nature in the flowering, sprouting plant that he experiences the being of the plant as full of mystery. The mystery is not reduced to fragments, of course, nor is the dust brushed off the butterfly's wings. But our instinctive delight in the plant is raised to a higher level when not only the physical plant is seen but also that wonderful working of the gnomes' world below, with its immediate understanding that gives rise to intelligence, the gnomes' world which first pushes the plant upwards. Just as the human intellect is not subject to gravity, just as the head is carried without our feeling its weight, so the gnomes with the light of their intellect over-come what is of the earth and push the plant upwards. They prepare life down below. But the life would die away were it not given impetus by the chemical activity brought to it by the undines. And this must be imbued with light.

And so we picture, from below upwards, in bluish, blackish shades the force of gravity, to which an upward impulse is given by the gnomes, and flitting all around the plant – indicated by the leaves – the undine power that blends and disperses substances as the plant grows upwards. From above downwards, from the sylphs, light is made to leave its imprint in the plant and moulds and creates the form which descends as an ideal form and is taken up by the maternal womb of the earth; moreover fire spirits flit around the plant and concen-trate cosmic warmth in the tiny seed points. This is sent down to the gnomes together with the seed power, so that down there they can cause the plants to arise out of fire and life.

And further we now see that essentially the earth is indebted for its power of repulsion and its density to the antipathy of the gnomes and undines towards amphibians and fishes. If the earth is dense, this density is due to the antipathy by means of which the gnomes and undines maintain their form. When light and warmth come down to earth, this is at the same time an expression of that power of sympathy, that sustaining power of sylph love, which is carried through the air, and to the sustaining sacrificial power of the fire spirits, which brings the power to bend down to what is below. So we may say that, over the face of the earth, earth density, earth magnetism and earth gravity, in their upwardly striving aspect, unite with the downward striving power of love and sacrifice. And in this interworking of the downwards streaming force of love and sacrifice and the upwards streaming force of density, gravity and magnetism, in this interworking, where the two streams meet, plant life develops on the surface of the earth. Plant life is an outer expression of the interworking of world love and world sacrifice with world gravity and world magnetism.

So now you have seen what matters when we direct our gaze to the plant world, which so enchants, uplifts and inspires us. Real insight can only be gained when our vision embraces the spiritual, the supersensible, as well as what is accessible to the physical senses. This enables us to correct the capital error of materialistic botany, that fertilization occurs above the earth. What occurs there is not the process of fertilization but the preparation of the male seed of heaven for what is being made ready as the future plant in the maternal womb of the earth.

IX. Elemental Spirits and the Animal Kingdom

Dornach, 3 November 1923

YESTERDAY I spoke to you about the other side of existence in the natural world, about the supersensible and invisible beings which accompany the beings and processes visible to the senses. An earlier, instinctive vision beheld the beings of the supersensible world as well as those in the world of the senses. Today, these beings have withdrawn from human view. The reason why this company of gnomes, undines, sylphs and fire spirits is not perceptible in the same way as animals, plants and so on is merely that man, in the present epoch of his earth evolution, is not in a position to unfold his soul and spirit without the help of his physical and etheric bodies. In the present situation of earth evolution man is obliged to depend on the etheric body for the purposes of his soul and on the physical body for the purposes of his spirit. The physical body which provides the instrument for the spirit, that is, the sensory apparatus, is not able to enter into communication with the beings that exist behind the physical world. It is the same with the etheric body, which man needs to develop as an ensouled being. Through this, if I may put it so, half of his earthly environment escapes him. He passes over everything connected with the elemental beings about which I spoke yesterday. The physical and the etheric body have no access to this world. We can gain an idea of what actually escapes human beings today when we realize what such gnomes, undines and so on actually are.

We have, you see, a whole host of lower animals – lower at the present time – that consist only of a soft mass, which live in the fluid element, and have nothing in the way of a skeleton to give them internal support. They are creatures which belong to the latest phase of the earth's development, creatures which only now, when the earth has already evolved, develop what man – the oldest earth being – already developed in his head structure during the time of Old Saturn. These creatures have not progressed so far as to produce the hardened substance in them that can become the supporting skeleton.

It is the gnomes which, in a spiritual way, make up in the world for what the lower orders of the animals up to the amphibians lack. This applies also to the fish, which have only the beginnings of a skeleton. These lower animal orders only become complete, as it were, through the fact that gnomes exist.

The relationships between beings in the world are very different, and something arises between these lower creatures and the gnomes which I yesterday called antipathy. The gnomes do not wish to become like these lower creatures. They are continually on the watch to protect themselves from assuming their form. As I described to you, the gnomes are extraordinarily clever, intelligent beings. With them intelligence is already implicit in perception; they are in every respect the antithesis of the lower animal world. And whereas they have the significance for plant growth which I described yesterday, in the case of the lower animal world they actually provide its complement. They supply what this lower animal world does not possess. This lower animal world has a dull consciousness; the gnomes have a consciousness of the utmost clarity. The lower creatures have no bony skeleton, no bony support; the gnomes bind together everything that exists by way of gravity and fashion their bodies from this volatile, invisible force, bodies which are, moreover, in constant danger of disintegrating, of losing their substance. The gnomes must ever and again create themselves anew out of gravity, because they continually stand in danger of losing their substance. Because of this, in order to save their own existence, the gnomes are constantly attentive to what is going on around them. No being is a more attentive observer on earth than a gnome. It takes note of everything, for it must know everything, grasp everything, in order to save its life. A gnome must always be wide awake; if it were to become sleepy, as people often do, this sleepiness would immediately cause its death.

There is a German saying of very early origin which aptly expresses this characteristic of the gnomes, in having always to remain attentive. People say: pay heed like a goblin. And the gnomes are goblins. So, if one wishes to make someone attentive, one says to him: pay heed like a gnome. A gnome is really an attentive being. If one could place a gnome as an object lesson on a front desk in every school classroom, where all could see it, it would be a splendid example for the children to follow.

The gnomes have yet another characteristic. They are filled with an absolutely unconquerable lust for independence. They trouble themselves little about one another and give their attention only to the world of their own surroundings. One gnome takes little interest in another. But everything else in this world around them, in which they live, this interests them exceedingly.

Now I told you that the human body really is a hindrance to our perceiving such folk as these. The moment it ceases to be this hindrance, these beings are there, just as the other beings of nature are there for ordinary vision. Anyone who comes so far as to experience in full consciousness his dreams on falling asleep is well acquainted with the gnomes. You need only recall what I recently published in *Das Goetheanum* on the subject of dreams.[38] I said that a dream in no way appears to ordinary consciousness in its true form, but wears a mask. Such a mask is worn by the dream that we have on falling asleep. We do not immediately escape from the experience of our ordinary day consciousness. Reminiscences well up, memory pictures from life; or we perceive symbols representing the internal organs – the heart as a stove, the lungs as wings – all in symbolic form. These are masks. If someone were to see a dream unmasked, if he were actually to pass into the world of sleep without the beings existing there being masked, then, at the moment of falling asleep, he would behold a whole host of goblins coming towards him. In ordinary consciousness man is protected from seeing these things unprepared, for they would terrify him. The form in which they would appear would actually be copy images of all the qualities in the individual concerned that work as forces of destruction. He would perceive all the destructive forces within him, all that continually destroys. These gnomes, if perceived unprepared, would be nothing but symbols of death. Man would be terribly alarmed by them if in ordinary consciousness he knew nothing about them and was now confronted by them on falling asleep. He would feel entombed by them – for this is how it would appear – entombed by them over yonder in the astral world. For it is a kind of entombment by the gnomes which, seen from the other side, takes place on falling asleep.

This holds good only for the moment of falling asleep. A further complement to the physical, sense-perceptible world are the undines, the water beings, which continually transform themselves, and which live in connection with water just as the gnomes live in connection with the earth. These undines – we have come to know the role they play in plant growth – exist as complementary beings to animals that are at a somewhat higher stage and have assumed a more differentiated earthly body. These animals, which have developed into the more evolved fish, or also into the more evolved amphibians, require scales, require some sort of hard external armour. The powers needed to provide certain creatures with this outer support, this outer skeleton – for these powers the world is indebted to the activity of the undines. The gnomes support spiritually the creatures which are at quite a low stage. The creatures which must be supported externally, which must be clad in a kind of armour, owe their protective armour to the activity of the undines. Thus it is the undines which impart to these somewhat higher animals in a primitive way what we have in the cranial part of the skull. They make them, as it were, into heads.

All the beings that are invisibly present behind the visible world have their great task in the great scheme of things. You will always notice that, where one wishes to use materialistic science to explain something of the kind I have just developed, there it breaks down. It cannot be used, for instance, to explain how the lower creatures, which are scarcely any more solid than the element in which they live, manage to propel themselves forward in it, because the scientists do not know about the spiritual support provided by the gnomes which I have just described. Equally, the development of external armour will always present a problem to purely materialistic scientists, because they do not know that the undines, in their sensitivity to, and avoidance of, their own tendency to become lower animals cast off what then appears on the somewhat higher animals as scales or some other kind of armour.

Again, in the case of these elemental beings, it is only the body which hinders the ordinary consciousness of today from seeing them just as it sees the leaves of plants, for example, or the somewhat higher animals.

When, however, man falls into a state of deep, dreamless sleep, and yet his sleep is not dreamless because through the gift of Inspiration it has become transparent, then his spiritual gaze perceives the undines rising up out of that astral sea in which, on falling asleep, he was engulfed, submerged by the gnomes. In deep sleep the undines become visible. Sleep extinguishes ordinary consciousness, but the sleep which is illumined by clear consciousness has as its content the wonderful world of ever-changing fluidity, a fluidity that rises up in all kinds of ways to create the metamorphoses of the undines. Just as for day consciousness we have around us beings with firm contours, a clear night consciousness would present to us these ever-changing beings, which themselves rise up and sink down again like the waves of the sea. All deep sleep is filled with a moving sea of living beings, a moving sea of undines all around the human being.

Matters are otherwise with the sylphs. In a way they also

complement the being of certain animals, but now in the other direction. The gnomes and undines add what is of the nature of the head to the animals where this is lacking. Birds, however, as I described to you, are actually pure head; they are entirely head organization. The sylphs add to the birds in a spiritual way what they lack as the physical complement of their head organization. They complement the bird kingdom in regard to what corresponds to the metabolism and limbs in man. If the birds fly about in the air with atrophied legs, so much the more powerfully developed is the limb system of the sylphs. They may be said to represent in the air, in a spiritual way, what the cow represents below in physical matter. This is why I was able to say yesterday that it is in connection with the birds that the sylphs have their ego, have what connects them with the earth. Man acquires his ego on the earth. What connects the sylphs with the earth, that is the bird kingdom. The sylphs are indebted to the bird kingdom for their ego, or at least for the consciousness of their ego.

Now when someone has slept through the night, has had around him the astral sea that gives rise to the most manifold undine forms, and then wakes up with an awakening dream, then again, if this dream on awakening were not masked in reminiscences of life or symbolic representations of the organs, if he were to see the unmasked dream, he would be confronted by the world of the sylphs. But these sylphs would assume for him a strange form; they would appear much as the sun might if it wished to send to human beings something which would affect them strangely, something which would lull them spiritually to sleep. We shall hear shortly why this is the case. Nevertheless, if someone were to perceive his unmasked dream on awakening, he would see light fluttering towards him, the essence of light fluttering towards him. He would find this an unpleasant experience, particularly also because the limbs of these sylphs would, as it were, spin and weave around him. He would feel as though the light were attacking him from all sides, as if the light were something that beset him and to which he was extraordinarily sensitive. Now and then he would perhaps also feel this to be like a caress from the light. But in all these things I only wish to indicate to you how the light, with its upholding, gently touching quality, actually approaches in the sylph's form.

When we come to the fire spirits, we find that they provide the complement to the fleeting nature of the butterflies. A butterfly itself develops as little as possible of its actual physical body; it lets this be as tenuous as possible. It is, on the contrary, a creature of light. The fire spirits appear as beings which complement the butterfly's body, so that we can get the following impression. If, on the one hand, we had a physical butterfly before us, and pictured it suitably enlarged, and on the other hand a fire spirit – they are, it is true, rarely together, except in the circumstances which I mentioned to you yesterday – then, if these two were welded together, we would get something resembling a winged human being, actually a winged human being. We need only increase the size of the butterfly, and adapt the size of the fire spirit to human proportions, and from this we would get something like a winged human being.

This again shows that the fire spirits are in fact the complement to the creatures that are nearest to what is spiritual; they complement them, so to say, in a downward direction. Gnomes and undines complement in an upward direction, towards the head; sylphs and fire spirits complement the birds and butterflies in a downward direction. Thus the fire spirits must be brought together with the butterflies.

Now in the same way that man can, as it were, penetrate the sleeping dream, so can he also penetrate waking day life. But here he makes use of his physical body in quite a robust way. This, too, I have described in essays in *Das Goetheanum*.[39] Here man is totally unable to realize that he could actually always see the fire spirits in his waking life, for the fire spirits are inwardly related to his thoughts, to everything which proceeds from the organization of the head. But when someone has progressed so far that he can remain completely in waking consciousness but nevertheless stand in a certain sense outside himself, viewing himself from outside as a thinking being while standing firmly on the earth, then he will become aware how the fire spirits are the element in the world which, when we perceive it, makes our thoughts perceptible from the other side.

Thus the perceiving of the fire spirits can enable man to *see* himself as thinker, not merely to *be* the thinker and, as such, hatch out thoughts, but actually to behold how the thoughts run their course. In that case, however, thoughts cease to be bound to the human being. They reveal themselves to be world thoughts; they are active and move as impulses in the world. Then one finds that the human head only calls forth the illusion that thoughts are enclosed inside the skull. They are only reflected there; their mirrored images are there. What underlies these thoughts belongs to the sphere of the fire spirits. On entering this sphere one sees thoughts to be not only what they are in themselves, but the thought content of the world, which, at the same time, is actually a content rich in images. The power to stand outside oneself is the power that enables one to arrive at the realization that thoughts are world thoughts.

I venture to add, when we behold what is to be seen upon the earth not from a human body but from the sphere of the fire spirits – that is, from the Saturn nature that projects into the earth, as it were – then we gain exactly the picture of the evolution of the earth which I have described in *Occult Science: An Outline*. This book is actually so composed that the thoughts appear as the thought content of the world seen from the perspective of the fire spirits.

You see, these things do have a deep and real significance. But they also have a deep and real significance for man in other ways. Take the gnomes and undines: they are, so to say, in the world which borders on human consciousness; they are already beyond the threshold. Ordinary consciousness is protected from seeing these beings, for the fact is that these beings are not all benevolent. The benevolent beings are, for instance, those which I described yesterday as working in the most varied ways on plant growth. But not all these beings are well disposed. And the moment one breaks through into the world where they are active, one finds there not only the well-disposed beings but the malevolent ones as well. One must first form a conception as to which of them are well disposed and which of them malevolent. This is not so easy, as you will see from the way I must describe the malevolent ones. The main difference between the ill-disposed beings and the well-disposed is that the latter are always drawn more to the plant and mineral kingdoms, whereas the ill-disposed are drawn to the animal and human kingdoms. Some, which are even more malevolent, then desire to approach the kingdoms of the plants and the minerals as well. But one can gain quite a fair idea of the malevolence which the beings of this realm can have, when one turns to those which are drawn to human beings and animals, wishing in particular to accomplish in man what is allotted by the Higher Hierarchies to the well-disposed beings for the plant and mineral world.

You see, there exist ill-disposed beings from the realm of the gnomes and undines that make for human beings and animals and cause the complement which they are supposed to add only to the lower animals to come to physical realization in human beings. This element is already present in man, but their aim is that it should be manifested physically in human beings – and also in animals. Through the presence of these malevolent gnome and undine beings, animal and plant life of a low order – parasites – live in human beings and in animals. These malevolent beings are the begetters of parasites. The moment man crosses the threshold of the spiritual world, he at once meets the trickery that exists in this world. Snares are everywhere, and he must first learn something from the goblins, namely, to be attentive. This is something that spiritualists, for example, can never manage!

Everywhere there are snares. Now someone might say: 'Why then are these malevolent gnome and undine beings there, if they engender parasites?' Well, if they were not there, man would never be able to develop within himself the power to evolve the brain substance. And here we meet something of extraordinary significance.

If you think of the human being as consisting of metabolism and limbs, of the chest, that is, the rhythmical system, and then the head, that is, the system of nerves and senses, there are certain things about which you must be quite clear. Down below processes are taking place – let us leave out the rhythmical sphere – and above processes are taking place. If you look at the processes taking place below as a whole, you find that in ordinary life they have one result that is usually disregarded. These processes are those of elimination – through the intestines, through the kidneys, and so on – all of them having their outlet in a downward direction. They are mostly regarded simply as processes of elimination. But this is nonsense. Elimination does not take place merely in order to eliminate, but to the same degree in which the products of elimination appear something appears spiritually in the lower man which resembles what the brain is physically above. What occurs in the lower man is a process which is arrested halfway in regard to its physical development. Elimination takes place because the process passes over into the spiritual. In the upper man the process is taken to its conclusion. What below is only spiritual there assumes physical form. Above we have the physical brain, below a spiritual brain. And if what is eliminated below were to be subjected to a further process, if one were to continue the transformation, then the final metamorphosis would, for the time being, be the human brain.

The human brain is the further evolved product of elimination. This is something which is of immense importance, in regard to medicine for instance, and it is something of which doctors in the sixteenth and seventeenth centuries were still fully aware. Of course today people speak in a very derogatory manner – and rightly in many respects – of the 'filth dispensed in the pharmacies of old'. But this is because they do not know that that filth still contained 'mummies' of the spirit. Naturally this is not intended as a glorification of what has figured as 'quackery' in the past centuries, but I am drawing attention to many truths which have connections as deep as those which I have just cited.

The brain is a higher metamorphosis of the products of elimination. Hence the connection between diseases of the brain and intestinal diseases, and also their cure.

You see, because gnomes and undines exist, because there is a world in which they are able to live, the forces exist that are certainly capable of giving rise to parasites if proceeding from the lower man, but yet, at the same time, bring about in the upper man the metamorphosis of the products of elimination into the brain. It would be absolutely impossible for us to have a brain if the world were not so ordered that gnomes and undines can exist.

What holds good for gnomes and undines in regard to the destructive powers – for destruction and disintegration also proceed in their turn from the brain – this holds good for sylphs and fire spirits in regard to the constructive powers. Here again the well-disposed sylphs and fire spirits keep away from men and animals, and busy themselves with plant growth in the way I have indicated; but there are also those which are malevolent. These ill-disposed beings are above all concerned in carrying what should only have its place up above in the regions of air and warmth down into the watery and earthy regions.

Now if you wish to study what happens when these sylph beings carry what belongs up above down into the watery and earthy regions, look at the deadly nightshade *(Atropa bella-donna)*. This plant, if I may put it so, has been kissed in its flower by the sylph, and what could be beneficent juices have been changed into juices which are poisonous.

Here you have what may be called a displacement of spheres. It is right when the sylphs develop their enveloping forces up above, as I have already described, where the light literally comes and touches you all over – for the bird world needs this. But if the sylph descends, and makes use in the plant world below of what it should employ up above, a potent vegetable poison is engendered. Parasitic beings arise through gnomes and undines, and through sylphs the poisons which are in fact a heavenly element that has streamed down too far and reached the earth. When people or certain animals eat the fruit of the deadly nightshade, which looks like a cherry, except that it conceals itself in the calyx (it is pushed down – you can see what I have just described when you look at the plant) – when people or certain animals eat the berry, it is fatal to them. But just look at the thrushes and blackbirds; they perch on the plant and get from it the best food in the world. It is to their region that what is present in the belladonna belongs.

It is a remarkable thing that the animals and man who in their lower organs are in fact earthbound should experience as poison what has become corrupted on the earth in the deadly nightshade, whereas birds such as thrushes and blackbirds, which should really get this in a spiritual way from the sylphs – and indeed through the benevolent sylphs do so obtain it – are able to assimilate it even when what belongs up above in their region has been carried down to the earth. They find nourishment in what is poison for beings more bound to the earth. Thus you get a conception of how, on the one side, through gnomes and undines what is of a parasitic nature strives upwards from the earth towards other beings, and of how the poisons filter downwards from above.

When, on the other hand, the fire beings imbue themselves with the impulses that belong in the region of the butterflies, and are of great use to them in their development – when the fire beings carry those impulses down into the fruits, there arise the poisonous almonds that are found in some species of almond. The poison is carried into the fruit of the almond trees through the activity of the fire beings. And yet the fruit of the almond could not come into existence at all if those same fire beings did not in a beneficial way burn, as it were, what is the edible part in other fruits. Only look at the almond. With other fruits you have the white kernel at the centre and around it the flesh of the fruit. With the almond you have the kernel there in the centre, and around it the flesh of the fruit is quite burnt up. That is the activity of the fire beings. And if this activity miscarries, if what the fire beings are bringing about is not confined to the brown shell, where their activity can still be beneficial, and something of what should be engaged in developing the shell penetrates into the white kernel, then the almond becomes poisonous.

And so you have gained a picture of the beings which are in the world lying immediately beyond the threshold, and of how, if they follow their impulses, they become the bearers of parasitic and poisonous principles, and therewith of illnesses. Now it becomes clear how far man in health raises himself above the forces that take hold of him in illness. For illness springs from the malevolence of these beings who are necessary for the upbuilding of the world of nature, for its shooting and sprouting growth – but also for its fading and decay.

These are the things which, arising from instinctive clairvoyance, underlie such Intuitions as those of the Indian Brahma, Vishnu and Shiva. Brahma represented the active being in the world sphere which may legitimately approach man. Vishnu represented the world sphere which may only approach man in so far as what has been built up must again be broken down, in so far as it must be continually transformed. Shiva represented everything connected with the forces of destruction. And in the earlier stages of the flower of Indian civilization it was said: 'Brahma is intimately related to all that is of the nature of the fire spirits and the sylphs, Vishnu with all that is of the nature of sylphs and undines, Shiva with all that is of the nature of undines and gnomes.' Generally speaking, when we go back to these more ancient conceptions, we find everywhere the pictorial expressions for what must be sought today as lying behind the secrets of nature.

Yesterday we studied the connection of these invisible folk with the plant world; today we have added their connection with the world of the animals. Everywhere beings on this side of the threshold are interlocked with those from beyond it; as are beings from beyond the threshold with those on this side. Only when one knows the living interaction of both these kinds of being does one really understand how the visible world unfolds. Knowledge of the supersensible world is indeed very, very necessary for man, for the moment he passes through the gate of death he no longer has the sense-perceptible world around him, but initially this other world begins to be his world. At his present stage of evolution man cannot find right access to the other world unless he has recognized in physical manifestations the written characters which point to this other world, unless he has learned to read in the creatures of the earth, in the creatures of the water, in the creatures of the air and in what I would like to call the creatures of the light, the butterflies, what points to the elemental beings which are our companions between death and a new birth. What we see of the creatures here between birth and death is, so to speak, their crude, dense part. We only learn to recognize what belongs to them as their supersensible nature when, with insight and understanding, we enter into this supersensible world.

X. Ahrimanic Elemental Beings

Torquay, 19 August 1924

WHEN WE develop the levels of consciousness of which I have already spoken, then each particular level opens the door to a specific cosmic sphere. I propose to describe in outline the relationship between the nature of man's perception and the different spheres to which we can attain by developing the appropriate conditions of consciousness. Of course I can only depict these spheres as contiguous, although, in reality, they interpenetrate. I have already shown how the Moon and Mercury spheres permeate our own sphere.

Let us suppose we develop the level of consciousness which enables us to be in touch with the dead in the years immediately after their death. This world borders on our world.

The next level of consciousness by means of which we penetrate further into the life of the deceased after he has retraced his earthly life in reverse order (in kamaloka) is that which I have called the emptied consciousness, but a waking consciousness in relation to the physical world. We then enter into a wider realm where we are intimately associated with the Mercury beings, with the events and occurrences characteristic of the sphere of Raphael. Here we become aware especially of the healing forces inherent in human nature.

Thus with each state of consciousness we enter into a specific region of the universe, and so we learn to know the beings who belong to these regions at any particular time. If we wish to inform ourselves of the conditions under which human beings live immediately after death, we must develop the appropriate consciousness in order to enter the world in which they dwell. Their true form is only revealed to us in the world to which they belong. If we wish to observe the Mercury beings we must share the consciousness of their world. Thus we can take it for granted that these worlds are, in a certain sense, insulated from each other and that each world has its specific condition of consciousness. Indeed, if we would understand the universe aright, this is a prerequisite, for only in this way can we prepare ourselves to know these beings in their true character. I propose to show you by means of a simple example in what direction such knowledge leads – a knowledge that seeks to develop in the right way the state of consciousness appropriate to a particular cosmic sphere.

Let us assume we have before us a plant with its leaves and flowers. We have already learned that a plant is the reflected image of the archetypal form existing in the spiritual world and which forms the plant-being on earth. And when we gain knowledge of the plant kingdom by raising our consciousness into this world of archetypal forms, something of vital importance is disclosed, namely, that we must clearly differentiate between the kinds of plants found on earth. When we examine a particular specimen, the *Cichorium intybus* (chicory), for example, with the appropriate spiritual perception, its appearance is different from that of many others. Let us take a typical example, the common violet and compare it with *Belladonna,* the deadly nightshade. When we study the plant kingdom in the way I have indicated, we shall find, when we participate in the world to which the violet belongs, that is, in the world of the emptied, waking consciousness, that the violet stands revealed in all its innocence to the eye of the spirit.

The deadly nightshade, *Belladonna,* on the other hand, derives its being from other worlds. We understand the being of the common plant when we perceive that it possesses a physical and etheric body and that the flowers and fruit are surrounded by the universal cosmic element. We see the organic life of the plant sprouting everywhere out of the earth, the etheric body around it and the astral element seemingly enveloped in cloud. Such is the nature of plants like the violet. Plants like the deadly nightshade have a different arrangement. The *Belladonna* develops its bell-shaped flowers inside which the fruit is formed and the astral element penetrates into the fruit. The violet develops its capsule only in the etheric element. The fruit of the deadly nightshade assimilates the astral element and in consequence the plant is poisonous. All plants which in any of their parts assimilate astrality from out of the cosmos are poisonous. Those forces which enter into the animal, provide it with an astral body and fashion it inwardly into a sentient being are also the source of the toxic element in plants.

This is most interesting. We find that our astral body is the bearer of forces which prove to be poisonous when assimilated by plants. This is how we must think of poison. We can only acquire an inner understanding of poison when we realize that man's astral body contains in effect the forces of all existing toxins, for they are an integral part of his being.

In this discussion I simply wish to present a clear-cut point of view which will be of service later in helping us to distinguish between true and false paths in spiritual investigation. What do we learn from the examples of the violet and belladonna? When we have developed the consciousness appropriate to the world of each plant we perceive that the violet is a being that remains within the world proper to it and attracts to itself nothing from a world that is alien to it. The deadly nightshade, on the other hand, attracts to itself something from an alien world; it assimilates something that is the prerogative of the animal kingdom and not the plant kingdom. This is true of all poisonous plants. They assimilate something which should not belong to the being of the plant, but which belongs in reality to the animal kingdom.

Now in the cosmos there are many beings belonging to different regions. In the region where we meet with the dead and can follow them for 10, 20 or 30 years after their death until they leave this region, are to be found a number of beings who are undoubtedly real, but who, unperceived by people, enter into our physical world. Perhaps I can best describe them as a particular kind of elemental being. When, therefore, we follow the dead after they have passed through the gates of death, we enter into a world inhabited by all kinds of elemental beings who are endowed with form and who really belong to that world. We may say therefore that, since these beings appertain to that world, they ought in reality to utilize only the forces pertaining to it. Now amongst these elemental beings will be found some who do not confine their activities to their own world, but who observe people when they write, for example, and who follow all the activities within the world of human beings between birth and death. We are permanently surrounded by such beings who are spectators of our activities.

Now this spectator role is not in itself harmful, for the essence of the entire plan underlying what I am now describing is that all the worlds which border on our own, the world we enter immediately after death, the world where we contact the dead many decades after death, all these worlds lack everything that man acquires through his association with the physical world. In this world of the dead there is, for example, neither writing nor reading; there are no aeroplanes, no motor cars or coaches-and-four as we know them.

We cannot say that here on earth we construct motor cars, write, read and write books, in all of which angels do not also participate. We cannot say that all these things have no significance for the cosmos in general. The fact is that those beings which I have just described are 'commissioned' from the world immediately adjacent to our own. They have to keep an eye on the activities of man. From other worlds they are charged with the mission to concern themselves with human nature and to preserve what they learn in that field for future times.

As human beings we are able to carry over our karma from one life to the next and also the effects of external culture upon our karma. We can carry over from one earthly life to another our experiences associated with the motor car, but not the construction of the car itself. We cannot ourselves carry over from one life to the next that which is born of earthly forces alone. In the course of civilization, therefore, mankind has laid the foundations of something that would be lost to it if other beings had not come to its aid. Now the beings of whom I have spoken are 'detailed' for the task of preserving for the future that which man cannot carry over from one earthly life to another.

Since in past ages it has been most difficult for many of these beings to fulfil their tasks, much of what had been discovered in ancient times has again been lost to humanity. The salient point I am trying to establish is that we are surrounded by beings who, in accordance with the cosmic plan, have been charged with the mission to carry over into the future that which man himself is unable to transmit from one earthly life to another, especially the abstract content of our libraries, for example. The spiritual beings with whom man is in direct contact cannot do it and therefore we as human beings cannot do it either. These beings must enlist into their service others who had long been alien to them, who had experienced a totally different evolution from the spiritual beings associated with man. These beings with their different evolution I have called in my books ahrimanic beings. Despite their different evolution there are occasions when they come in contact with our own, when, for example, we build a motor car. They are beings who are able by virtue of their ahrimanic cosmic forces to understand modern techniques such as the construction of a motor car. They transmit to future ages the technical achievements of civilization which man himself cannot carry over from one incarnation to the next.

With this information at our disposal we are now in a position to describe what a medium really is. We must of course distinguish between a medium in the widest sense and a medium in the literal sense of the word. Taking the term 'medium' in the widest sense, we are all mediums fundamentally. We are all beings of soul and spirit before we incarnate to live out our life between birth and death. Our spiritual essence is incarnated in the physical body. The physical body is an intermediary for the activities of the spirit. Taking the word 'medium', then, in the widest sense, we can say that every being is to some extent a medium. This is not the meaning we attach to the term 'a mediumistic type' in the normal sense. In the world between birth and death a mediumistic person is one who has developed certain sectors of the brain in such a way that they can be isolated from his total being. Thus, at certain times, those parts of the brain which sustain the ego-activity in particular no longer serve as a basis for this ego-activity.

When we say 'I' to ourselves, when we are fully ego-conscious, this consciousness is rooted in specific parts of the brain. These parts of the brain are insulated by the medium and, instead of the human ego, certain entities of the class I have just described feel an urge to slip into these parts of the brain. Such a medium then becomes the vehicle of those beings whose real function is to transmit to the future the achievements of civilization. When these entities take possession of a brain from which, at certain times, the ego is absent, they feel an overwhelming desire to establish themselves in this brain. And when a medium is in a trance condition, when the brain is insulated, an entity of this kind which is subject to ahrimanic influences and whose function is to transmit the achievements of civilization to the future slips into the brain. Instead of being the bearer of the human ego, such a medium is, temporarily, the vehicle of an elemental being which is neglecting its duty in the cosmos. I want you to take quite literally the expression: a being which is neglecting its duty in the cosmos.

The duty of such a being is to observe how people write. Human beings write with the forces which are rooted in those parts of the brain of which I am speaking. Instead of merely observing, as is the normal practice, these beings are on the look-out at all times for a mediumistic brain that can be insulated. Then they slip into it and introduce into the contemporary world what their observation has taught them of the art of writing. Thus, with the help of mediums they project into the present that which, in accordance with their mission, they ought to communicate to the future. Mediumism depends upon the fact that what is to become future capacities is already developed in the present in a vague and chaotic manner. This is the origin of the prophetic gift of the medium and the fascination he has for others. Indeed its operations are more perfect than those of man today, but it is introduced by beings in the manner already described.

Just as the *Belladonna* mediates the astral world – acts as a medium for certain astral forces that it absorbs into its fruit – so a human being through his particular type of brain is a medium for these elemental beings who at some future time must participate in our civilization, because human beings cannot carry over everything from one earthly life to another. This is the real secret of mediumship – possession by a certain class of beings.

Now you may conclude that these beings are, on the one hand, actual creations of ahrimanic beings. Ahrimanic beings exist in the cosmos and possess an intelligence far superior to that of mankind. When we encounter the ahrimanic beings in the world immediately adjacent to our own or, having attained insight, encounter them in the physical world as well, we are astonished at their vast, outstanding intelligence. Their intelligence ranges far beyond that of human kind. And we first learn to respect them when we realize how infinitely intelligent they are. Something of this intelligence passes over to their progeny, the elemental beings who slip into mediumistic brains, so that in this way significant information may be revealed by mediums. We may learn much of capital importance, especially if we attend in fully developed consciousness to what they communicate. When we rightly understand the nature and constitution of the spiritual world, we cannot deny that mediums are able to impart much authentic information. Though we may learn much of importance from them, this is not the right path to spiritual knowledge.

You will realize this from the example of plants which are

plant mediums, mediums for certain astral forces which are responsible for the toxicity in plants. It is only through a rightly developed consciousness that we realize how this situation arose. I should like to describe this in the following way, for when discussing the spiritual world it is better to provide a clear, concrete description than to deal in abstract concepts.

Let us assume that with initiation-knowledge we enter into the world where the dead live in their life after death. When we accompany the dead in this way we first enter into a world totally different from our own. I have already described it to some extent and have pointed out that it gives an impression of far greater reality than the world in which we live between birth and death.

When we enter this world we are astonished at the remarkable beings to be found there, apart from the souls of the dead. The souls of those who have recently died are surrounded by strange demonic forms. At the entrance to this intermediate world which the dead must enter and in which we can accompany them with a certain clairvoyant vision, we meet with demonic figures with enormous webbed feet – enormous by earthly standards – like the duck or the wild duck species and other aquatic animals, huge webbed feet that are perpetually changing shape. These beings have a form somewhat similar to that of the kangaroo, but half bird, half mammal. And when we accompany the dead we pass through vast areas where such beings dwell.

If we ask ourselves where these beings are to be found, we must first have a clear idea of the location of such beings, of where we imagine them to exist. They are always around us, for we inhabit the same world as the dead, but you must not look for them in this hall. It is at this point that the path to real and exact investigation begins.

Suppose you are walking through a meadow where many plants of the species *Colchicum autumnale,* the autumn crocus, are to be found. If, as you are standing among the autumn crocuses, you try to evoke the state of consciousness that is able to follow the dead, you will see, wherever an autumn crocus is growing, a being of the kind I have just described, with webbed feet and strange kangaroo-like body. Such a being emerges from every autumn crocus.

If you were to move on to another area where the *Belladonna*, the black deadly nightshade, grows by the roadside, and if you transpose yourself into the state of consciousness of which I have spoken, you will meet with totally different beings horrible, demonic beings who also belong to this world. *Colchicum autumnale* and *Belladonna* therefore are mediums which permit beings of the next world to enter into them and which in their other aspect really belong to the world of the dead.

If we bear this in mind, we shall realize that everywhere around us is another world. It is essential that we should enter this world consciously, that we should perceive the *Colchicum autumnale* and the *Belladonna* not solely with the normal consciousness but with the higher consciousness that is in touch with the dead.

Now consider the following. Here is a meadow, we will suppose, where the autumn crocuses are growing. In order to find the plants that bear the *Belladonna* flowers you might have to travel far and climb a mountainside. On the physical plane, *Belladonna* and autumn crocus are not found together. But in the spiritual world they are found in close proximity. Space is of a different order. Objects that may be situated far apart in the physical world may be in close proximity in the spiritual world. The spiritual world has its own primordial laws; there everything is different.

Now suppose we meet with these plants in the world of the dead. When we are first in touch with the dead, we discover that these plants by no means evoke in them the horrible impression they evoke in us. They, the deceased, know that the presence of these demonic beings is in accordance with a wise cosmic plan. When therefore we are in touch with the dead, we find that the intermediate world is populated with demonic forms corresponding to the poisonous plants. If we then progress further towards the realms from which the dead withdraw after 10, 20 or 30 years in order to enter into a higher realm, we find the related forms of the non-poisonous plants. Thus the plant kingdom plays a significant part both in the physical and the next higher world. In the latter, however, it assumes different forms.

That which belongs in its true form to the world of the stars has its counterpart on earth in the form of a *Belladonna*, an autumn crocus or a violet. It has also its counterpart in the world of the dead where its true form is reflected in the manner already described. Everything in the one world reacts upon the other worlds. But in order to have real knowledge of these things we must enter consciously into the world where they really belong.

The same applies to the beings of these other worlds. We can only know what the elemental beings are, the progeny of the ahrimanic powers, when we enter into the world immediately bordering on our own. Now these beings manifest through mediums. They take possession of the mediums and in this way temporarily enter our world. If we contact them through a human medium only, we learn to know them in a world that should really be foreign to them; we do not know them in their true form. Therefore those who learn to know them only by their manifestations through mediums cannot possibly arrive at the truth since these beings are manifesting in a world that is foreign to them. Spiritual revelations are undoubtedly transmitted, but it is impossible to understand them when they issue from a world to which they do not belong. The deceptive and highly hallucinatory element in everything connected with mediumistic consciousness is explained by the fact that those who contact these beings have no understanding of their real nature.

Now because they enter the world in this way a unique destiny is reserved to these beings. The knowledge of the universe that I have described serves to enlarge our field of knowledge. When we enter the world of the dead and traverse the demonic forest of *Colchicum autumnale, Digitalis purpurea*

(purple foxglove), *Datura stramonium* (thorn-apple) and so
on, we realize that violets will undergo a metamorphosis and
in future will assume totally different forms. They have a
significance for the future of the cosmos. By its very nature the
autumn crocus prepares the death for which it is destined.
The poisonous plants are moribund plants, species that are
dying out, with no possibility of future development. In future
times they will be replaced by other poisonous species. The
poisonous species of today are already dying out in our epoch.
The epoch of course is of long duration, but these poisonous
plants have the seeds of death within them. And this will be
the fate of all vegetation. When we survey the world of
vegetation with this spiritual vision we perceive forces of
growth and development with a dynamic urge towards the
future and a world that is dying and doomed to perish.

And so it is with the beings who take possession of the
mediums. They detach themselves from their companions
whose task is to carry over the present into a distant future.
Through the agency of mediums they invade the world of the
present, are there caught up in the destiny of the earth and
sacrifice their future mission. In this way they deprive man to
a large extent of his future mission. And this is what faces us
when we understand the real nature of mediumism, for
mediumism implies that the future shall perish in order that
the present may be all important. When therefore we attend
a seance with insight into the real occult relationships and into
the true nature of the cosmos, we are at first astonished to find
that the entire circle participating in a spiritistic manifestation
is seemingly surrounded by poisonous plants. Every
spiritualistic seance is surrounded in fact by a garden of
poisonous plants that no longer bear the same aspect as in the
kingdom of the dead but which grow up around the spiritu-
alist circle, and from their fruits and flowers demonic beings
are seen to emerge.

Such is the experience of the clairvoyant at a spiritualistic
seance. For the most part he goes through a kind of cosmic

thicket of poisonous plants that are activated from within and are part animal. Only by their forms do we recognize that they are poisonous plants. We learn from this how everything at work within this mediumistic form that ought to advance the course of human evolution and bear fruit in the future is relegated to the present where it does not belong. In the present, it works to the detriment of humanity.

Such is the inner mystery of mediumism, a mystery of which we shall learn more in the course of these lectures.

It is now possible to indicate precisely what aspect of mediumism presents a major problem to the constitution of man. In this context my account must of necessity appear somewhat abstract, but it will help you a little towards some understanding of the nature of mediumism.

Now the human brain lying in the cranial cavity has an average weight of 1500 grams or a little more. That is really a considerable weight, and if the human brain were to press with its own weight on the delicate veins at the base of the brain, they would immediately be crushed. However long we live, the weight of our brain never presses upon the network of veins beneath it. We understand this immediately if we interpret it in the right way. Let us take man as he is at present constituted. The spinal canal passes upwards and terminates in the brain. With the exception of certain portions, the spinal canal is filled with fluid and the brain floats in this fluid.

Now let us consider the law of Archimedes. You will be familiar with it from your study of physics. It is said that he discovered it in a flash of inspiration while he was in his bath. He made the following experiment: with his body wholly immersed in the bath he lifted first one leg and then the other out of the water. He noted that his legs had a different weight according to whether they were in the water or out of it. They lost weight when they were immersed in the water. For a person such as Archimedes this experience had wider implications. He discovered that when an object is wholly immersed in a fluid the apparent loss of weight is equal to the weight of water displaced.

A beaker filled with water is placed on a bench and a solid body suspended by a thread from the hook of a spring balance is lowered into the water. We find that the weight of the body is less in water than in air. When a solid body is immersed in a fluid it experiences an upthrust equal to the weight of the fluid displaced. This is the law of Archimedes.

And this principle is of great benefit to man for the brain floats in the cerebral fluid; the apparent loss in weight of the brain is equal to the weight of the cerebral fluid displaced. Thus our brain does not weigh 1500 grams. Its loss in weight is equal to the weight of the fluid displaced, that is, 1480 grams, so that in accordance with the law of Archimedes its effective weight is only 20 grams approximately.

In our brain organization we have something that is much lighter than its real weight. Our brain weighs only 20 grams, but we must treasure these 20 grams for they alone can harbour our ego.

Now our whole body contains all manner of solid constituents which also float in a fluid medium – the blood corpuscles, for example. They all suffer loss of weight and only a fraction of their weight remains. They also harbour the ego. Thus the ego is diffused in the blood that is not subject to gravity. In the course of our life we must carefully observe everything within us that has perceptible weight. We must pay the strictest attention to what is situated in the heavy part of the brain and which still possesses weight in the literal sense. For there and nowhere else our ego may be situated – otherwise astral body, etheric body and so on, take over.

The medium is a human being in whom this solid part of his constitution, the 20 gram brain, no longer contains the ego. The ego is expelled from those parts which still retain weight and then elemental beings can enter immediately.

A materialistic mode of thinking seeks to localize everything and wants to know in which part of the human being the elemental being is situated when it takes possession of the medium. This is the language of the materialistic mind that thinks mechanically and mathematically. Life, however, does not proceed mechanically or mathematically, but dynamically. We must not say, therefore, that the medium is possessed at some place or other that can be localized purely mathematically and geometrically. We must say: the medium is possessed in those parts of his constitution that possess weight or gravity, in the part that is attracted to the earth. There the ahrimanic beings can enter; and not only there, but also elsewhere. This description that I have presented to you gives only the crudest aspect of the matter. We have yet to discuss a more subtle aspect.

Now the eye is our organ of vision for the external world. The optic nerve, distributed in the eye, is connected with the brain and provides the basis for colour sensation. The materialist tries to explain how the optic nerve transmits the colour sensations to the brain and releases them there. He compares the whole process to the loading of a ship or a railway truck. Something is 'loaded into' the optic nerve from without and is transported by the nerves; it is then unloaded somewhere or other and then passes into the soul. The explanation is not quite as crude as this, but that is what it amounts to. The real explanation, however, is totally different.

The function of the optic nerve is not to convey the colour sensation backwards to the brain, but to insulate it at a certain point. The colour exists only at the periphery. The function of the optic nerve is to insulate the colour sensation the nearer it approaches the brain, so that the brain is virtually without colour sensations; only weak, faint colours reach the brain. And not only is colour sensation insulated, but also every kind of relationship to the external world. Hearing and sight are associated with the sense organs. In the proximate area of the brain the optic and auditory nerves and the nerves that register sensation of warmth reduce everything lying at the periphery to a dim impression. This bears the same relationship to the sensation as the 20 grams to the 1500 grams, for the 20 grams give only a faint impression of the weight of the brain. This is all that remains to us. When we take in the magnificent spectacle of the dawn through our senses, the hind-brain registers only a faint shadow, a dim impression of it. We must pay heed to this dim shadow, for it is only there that our ego can enter.

The moment our ego is insulated and we manifest mediumistic powers, an elemental being slips into this faint shadow or into the feeble tones that proceed from the auditory sense. This being slips into the parts vacated by the ego where the external sense-perception is obliterated, and takes possession of the medium. Then it enters into the ramifications of the nerves, into the will-organization – that is to say, the nerves that govern the formation of the will. In consequence the medium begins to respond actively because that which should be under the control of the ego has been taken over by the elemental being. All the subtle, shadowy elements, the residual weight of the brain, the remnants of the colour and auditory sensations, possess us like a phantom – for this 20 grams weight is only a phantom and these feeble shadows of the colours that penetrate into our inner being are phantom-like. The elemental being enters into this phantom and then the medium grows so lethargic that his body becomes wholly passive and everything in the dim, phantom-like shadows that should really be permeated by the ego – shadows that are normally tenanted by the ego – now becomes active within him.

A human being can only be a medium when he permits his faculties which are at the service of the normal person to be inhibited by lethargy, by total inertia, and when the phantom that I have described becomes activated. We can observe this, for example, in the way the medium writes. The medium, of course, could not write unless everything within him were lighter as in the case of the brain, for everything possessed of weight floats in a fluid medium, gives a feeling, a sensation of lightness and so the elemental being writes in those areas which are not subject to gravity and where normally the ego directs the pen. In the medium, then, it is the elemental being that takes over the direction of the pen in this human phantom.

There is no denying the fact that in all mediumistic phenomena we see the intrusion of another world. Just as the ahrimanic beings of another world can enter into the movements performed by the medium, so too can they enter into the emanations which I described yesterday. Powerful fluid emanations are present notably in the glandular regions of the human organization. These elemental beings penetrate not only into the fluid emanations but also into the breath emanations and light emanations. Only in the case of the chemical emanations is there conscious intercourse between the individual who makes use of these chemical emanations and the beings who enter into them. At this point black magic sets in – the conscious co-operation with these beings who enter in after the manner I have described.

Mediums and those who experiment with mediums are unaware of the real processes involved. The black magician, however, is fully conscious that he is invoking for his own purposes these beings of the elemental world into the chemical emanations of human beings, more especially into his own. Hence the black magician is perpetually surrounded by a host of subordinates consisting of these elemental beings, and he makes it possible for them to use the occult-chemical impulses in the phenomenal world, either through his own emanations or through fumigations, perfumes from the burning of aromatic gums carried out in his laboratory.

Thus we learn that just as the *Belladonna* trespasses into an alien world and so becomes toxic, so too through mediumship the spiritual world trespasses into the world we inhabit between birth and death. And fundamentally this danger is always present whenever the consciousness of man, i.e. his full ego-consciousness, is suppressed, whenever he is in a stupefied, comatose condition or has actually suffered syncope. Whenever man's consciousness is damped down, not through sleep, but through some other factor, there is the danger that man will be exposed to the world of elemental beings.

XI. The Elemental World and the Future of Mankind

Dornach, 28 May 1922

TODAY I want to bring forward certain matters which concern mankind's evolution in so far as this evolution is dependent upon man's relationship with certain spiritual powers during the earth's future.

We have seen how it is possible, through exact observation, to gain insight into the fact that within the physical-soul-spiritual being of man something comes together which, in a certain sense, belongs to the external world, in so far as this world consists of etheric forces and beings. Man draws together these forces to form his etheric body as he descends to earthly life. We see also that with this entity, consisting of forces from the external etheric world, there unites the effect of man's earthly deeds, of everything he causes to happen – in short, his karma.

I have often mentioned that a new stream of spirituality is now ready to pour into man's earthly existence. The present forms a link in mankind's evolution between an era of mainly intellectual development – which began in the first third of the fifteenth century and has now practically run its course – and a future devoted to the spiritual. The most important task for mankind in the era of intellectuality was the development of reason through the investigation of external nature and the development of technology.

In this direction great and impressive results have been accomplished in recent centuries. However, it must be said that the intellect has begun to lose its creativity, though we still live with its heritage. The most creative period was from the time of Copernicus, Galileo and Giordano Bruno right up to the nineteenth century. Especially in western civilization the greatest intellectual achievements have been attained in recent centuries.

It is obvious, even to an external unbiased observation, that the intellect has lost some of its creative power. In general, mankind has no longer the same enthusiasm for intellectual accomplishments. Yet the practice of centuries continues through a certain cultural inertia. Thoughts run along the old grooves but the intellect brings nothing new of real importance to the fore. This is particularly noticeable in our young people. Not so long ago it was a real pleasure to listen to a young person who had studied some subject. It may not have applied to everyone but certainly to those who had achieved something; one was eager to hear what they had to say, and it was the same everywhere in western academic circles. But a change has come about in the last few decades; when a young person fresh from university speaks one is no longer curious about what he will say next. One is not curious because one knows it already; it comes out automatically; it is as if the brain itself has lost its vitality. One gets the feeling that the activity of the intellect has slid down from the head to some deeper region. That human intelligence has become something mechanical which no longer springs from the region of the head must be obvious even to external observation. This situation has come about because intelligence was originally a natural endowment which mankind was predestined to develop predominantly between the fifteenth and nineteenth centuries.

However, in order to fructify the developed intellect, a stream of spirituality from higher regions of world existence now seeks entry into the earthly life of mankind. Whether this will happen depends upon man opening his heart and soul to what thus seeks entry, through many doors, as it were, into the earthly world from the spiritual world. It will be necessary for man not only to become conscious once more of the spiritual in all nature, but able to perceive it.

Consider how in the older civilizations mankind in general perceived – in all the kingdoms of nature, in every star, in every moving cloud, in thunder and lightning – spirit and soul. On the background of this general consciousness the yoga exercises evolved. As I explained yesterday, the yogi attempted to penetrate to his own self. Through inner exercises he sought to attain what today is taken for granted because we are born with it: consciousness of the 'I', the feeling of selfhood. This the yogi had first to develop in himself.

But, my dear friends, it would be a great mistake to compare the ordinary consciousness of self that we have today with that of the yogi. It makes a difference whether something is achieved through one's own human effort or whether one simply has it. When, as was the case with the yogi, one first had to struggle to attain consciousness of self, then, through the inner effort, one was transported into the great universal laws; one participated in world processes. This is not the case when one is simply placed into the sphere of self-consciousness. To belong willy-nilly to a certain level of human evolution is not the same as attaining that level through inner exercises.

You will realize from what was said yesterday that mankind must gradually acquire knowledge in a different way; he must set his thought processes free from the breathing process. As I explained yesterday, this has the effect that thinking, by no longer being bound up with the subject, is able to unite itself with the rhythm of the external cosmos. We must go with our thinking out of ourselves into the external world, whereas the yogi crept into his inner being by hitching together, as it were, the systems of thought and breath. In so doing he identified himself with what his spirit-soul nature was able to experience on the waves of the inner rhythm of breathing. By contrast, we must give ourselves up to the world in order to participate in all the various rhythms which go through the mineral, plant, animal and human worlds right up to the realm of the Hierarchies. We must enter into, and live within, the rhythm of external existence. In this way mankind will again gain insight into that spiritual foundation of nature which external knowledge does not reach.

The sciences of physics, chemistry and biology which are pursued nowadays provide mankind with a vast amount of popular information. What they actually do is explain how sense observation, interpreted by the intellect, sees the world. But the time has come when mankind must rediscover what lies behind the knowledge provided by external observation and intellectual interpretation.

If one has in mind their physical aspect only, when speaking about the four elements of earth, water, air and fire, then it makes no difference whether one uses these terms or prefers the more recent ones of solid, liquid, aeriform bodies and conditions of heat. When they are referred to today, all one has in mind is how the physical substances within them are either combined or mixed, or else separated. However, it must be stressed that everything of a solid, earthen nature has as its foundation an elemental spirituality. Today's 'enlightened' people may laugh when reminded that older folks used to see gnomes in everything earthy. However, when knowledge is no longer obtained by means of combining abstract, logical thoughts, but by uniting ourselves through our thinking with the world rhythm, then we shall rediscover the elemental beings contained in everything of a solid earthy nature. The outstanding characteristic of these elemental begins dwelling in solid earth is cleverness, cunning, slyness – in fact, a one-sidedly developed intellect.

Thus, in the solid earth element live spiritual beings of an elemental kind who are very much more clever than human beings. Even a person of extreme astuteness intellectually is no match for these beings who, as supersensible entities, live in the realm of solid earth. One could say that just as man consists of flesh and blood so do these beings consist of cleverness, of super-cleverness. Another of their peculiarities is that they prefer to live in multitudes. When one is in a position to find out how many of these astute beings a suitable earthy object contains, then one can squeeze them out as if from a sponge – in a spiritual sense, of course – and out they flow in an endless stream. But counting these gnome-like beings is a difficult task. If one tries to count them as one would cherries or eggs – i.e., one, two, three – one soon notices that they will not be counted that way. When one has reached say three, then there are suddenly a lot more. So counting them as one would on the physical plane is no use; nor is any other form of calculation, for they immediately play tricks on you. Suppose one put two on one side and two on the other in order to say that twice two makes four. One would be wrong, for through their super-cunning they would appear as seven or eight, making out that two times two makes eight, or something like that. Thus these beings defy being counted. It must be acknowledged that the intellect developed by man in recent times is very impressive. But these super-intelligent beings show a mastery over the intellect even where it is merely a question of numbers.

The elemental beings dwelling in the fluid element – i.e., in water – have particularly developed what is, in man, his life of feeling and sensitivity. In this respect we humans are really backward compared with these beings. We may take pleasure in a red rose or feel enchanted when trees unfold their foliage. But these beings go with the fluid which as sap rises in the rose bush and participate in the redness of the blossoms. In an intimate way they share feelingly in the world processes. We remain outside of things with our sensitivity, whereas they are right inside the process themselves and share in them.

The elemental beings of air have developed to a high degree what lives in the human will. It is splendid that the analytical chemist discovers the atomic weight of hydrogen, oxygen and nitrogen, and that he finds out how hydrogen and oxygen combine into water to be further analysed or else how chloride of lime is analysed, and so on. But elemental spiritual beings are active behind all this, and it is essential that man should acquire insight into their characteristics. During the period in which man developed the intellect – as already mentioned, this was from the first third of the fifteenth century to the end of the nineteenth century – these elemental beings were pushed to one side, as it were. While the intellect played a creative part in man's cultural life there was not much they could do; and because the elemental beings dwelling in solids had, in a certain sense, to hold back and leave the intellect to man, they also held back the beings of water and air. But now we live at a time when the intellect has begun to decline within the civilized world; it is falling into decadence. If mankind does not become receptive to what streams towards him from the spiritual world, then the result of this dullness on man's part will be – and there are signs already of it happening – that these elemental beings will gather together to form a kind of union and place themselves under the leadership of the supreme intellectual power: Ahriman.

If it should happen that the elemental beings come under the guidance of Ahriman with the clear intention of opposing human evolution, then mankind would be unable to make further progress. The possibility would arise that the ahrimanic powers in union with the elemental beings would divert the earth from its intended course. The earth would not continue what is described in my *Occult Science: An Outline* as the Saturn-Sun-Moon-Earth evolution. The earth can only become what it was originally intended to become if man, in each epoch, tackles his task rightly.

One can see already how matters stand. Those who have reached a certain age know that formerly one gained insight into another human being's inner thoughts and feelings simply through normal conversation and exchange of ideas. One took it for granted that a person's reason and intellect resided in his head, and what was in the head would be conveyed through the spoken word. There are many people today who no longer take it for granted that reason is located in the head of many of their contemporaries; rather do they assume it to have slid further down. So instead of listening they now analyse. This is just one example from one misunderstood aspect of the whole problem. But I would say that when one starts to psychoanalyse people instead of just letting them talk, then that is in fact an admission that reason no longer resides in the head. It is assumed to have slid down into deeper regions of human nature and must be psychoanalysed to be brought up again to consciousness. In this age of a declining intellect there are already people who dislike it if one appeals to their intelligence; they prefer to be analysed. This is because they do not want to participate with the head in what their soul brings to light.

Nothing is achieved by looking at these things merely from an external point of view. To see clearly what is involved they must be considered – as we have just done – in the wider context of world evolution. Certain aspects of psychoanalysis may do some good. There are conditions which formerly were simply accepted but are no longer tolerated and must be cured. However, as so many cures are needed, physical ones do not suffice, so one resorts to psychological ones. Why this should be so must be seen in a wider context.

Superficially judged, there is no point in objecting to all the good reasons and beguiling arguments put forward by psychoanalysts, not even from the wider viewpoint of world evolution. People want to avoid seeing things in their wider context, though it would lead them to the recognition that a spiritual stream is seeking to enter our present civilization to replace the declining intellect.

What we have considered so far amounts to one aspect of what in the future threatens mankind. There is another aspect – just as the lower elements of earth, water and air are inhabited by elemental beings, so are the higher elements of light ether, chemical ether and life ether. However, these beings of the higher elements differ considerably from those of the lower ones. The beings of light, and particularly those of life, do not aim at becoming multitudes. The ones who strive the most to become multitudes are the beings of the earth element. The beings of the etheric element strive rather towards unity. It is difficult to differentiate them from one another; they do not express any individuality and rather strive to amalgamate.

Certain initiates in ancient times, through whom certain teachings of the Old Testament originated, turned their attention particularly towards the etheric elements. The strong tendency of these elements towards unification created an influence which resulted in the strict monotheism of Judaism.

The religion which is based on the worship of Jehovah originated mainly from a spiritual vision of the realm of the ethers. In this realm live spiritual beings who do not strive to separate from one another and become many individuals. Rather do they strive to grow together and disappear into one another; they seek to become a unity.

If these beings are disregarded by man – i.e., if he does not turn to spiritual knowledge and the insight that what exists up in the sky is not merely the physical sun, but that with the sun's warmth and light etheric beings stream down to earth – if man's comprehension stops at the external material aspect, then the possibility exists that these beings will unite with ahrimanic powers. In order for the earth to become what it was originally intended to become, man must wake up to the dangers that threaten from both sides – on the one hand, the danger that those beings who dwell in the lower elements will join forces with ahrimanic powers, and on the other, that the ahrimanic powers will unite with those of the higher elements in their striving for unity.

The significance of spiritual knowledge for man's earthly destiny cannot be emphasized too strongly. Unless man draws near to spiritual reality something completely different from what ought to happen will happen to the earth. No matter how far or how deeply our sophisticated sciences of physics and chemistry investigate the material world around us, the fact remains that what is investigated will all disappear along with earth existence itself. In the last resort, chemistry and physics have no value whatever beyond the earth. When the evolution of the earth comes to an end, all mineral substances will turn to dust and dissolve in the cosmos. Only what pertains to the plant, animal and human world will pass over to the Jupiter existence. Therefore, all the magnificent achievements of these sciences are related only to what is transitory. It is essential that knowledge is attained of that which endures beyond the earth.

As already mentioned, whatever physical laws are discovered, whatever is investigated concerning the atomic weight of individual elements or whatever chemical formulae are produced, all these things are concerned only with what has merely transient significance. Man must grow beyond earth existence through knowledge of the kind of things I have explained. These are matters of great import and significance.

XII. Perception of the Elemental World

Munich, 26 August 1913

WHEN SPEAKING about the spiritual worlds as we are doing in these lectures, we should keep the following well in mind: the clairvoyant consciousness which the human soul can develop in itself will change nothing in the nature and individuality of a person, for everything entering that consciousness was already long present in man's nature. Knowing a thing is not the same as creating it; a person learns only to perceive what is already there as a fact. Obvious as this is, it has to be said, for we must lead our thoughts to realize that the nature of the human being is hidden in the very depths of his existence; it can be brought up out of those depths only through clairvoyant cognition. It follows from this that the true, inmost nature of man's being cannot be brought to light in any other way than through occult knowledge. We can learn what a human being actually is not through any kind of philosophy but only through the kind of knowledge based on clairvoyant consciousness. To the observation we use in the sense world and to the understanding limited to the sense world, the being of man, the true, inmost nature of man, lies in hidden worlds. Clairvoyant consciousness provides the point of view from which the worlds beyond the so-called threshold have to be observed; in order to perceive and learn, quite different demands are made on it from those in the sense world. This is the most important thing: that the human soul should become more or less accustomed to the fact that the way of looking at and recognizing things that for the sense world is the correct and healthy one is not the only way.

Here I shall give the name elemental world to the first world that the soul of a human being enters on becoming clairvoyant and crossing the threshold. Only a person who wants to carry the habits of the sense world into the higher supersensible worlds can demand a uniform choice of names for all the points of view the higher worlds can offer.

Fully new demands meet the life of soul when it steps over the threshold into the elemental world. If the human soul insisted on entering this world with the habits of the sense world, two things might happen: cloudiness or complete darkness would spread over the horizon of the consciousness, over the field of vision, or else – if the soul wanted to enter the elemental world without preparing itself for the peculiarities and requirements there – it would be thrown back again into the sense world. The elemental world is absolutely different from the sense world. In this world of ours when you move from one living being to another, from one happening to the next, you have these beings and events before you and can observe them; while confronting and observing them, you keep your own distinct existence, your own separate personality. You know all the time that in the presence of another person or happening you are the same person that you were before and that you will be the same when you confront a new situation; you can never lose yourself in another being or happening. You confront them, you stand outside them and you know you will always be the same in the sense world wherever you go.

This changes as soon as a person enters the elemental world. There it is necessary to adapt one's whole inner life of soul to a being or event so completely that one transforms one's own inner soul life into this other being, into this other event. We can learn nothing at all in the elemental world unless we become a different person within every other being, indeed unless we become similar, to a high degree, to the other beings and events.

We have to have, then, one peculiarity of soul for the elemental world: the capacity for transforming our own being into other beings outside ourselves. We must have the faculty of metamorphosis. We must be able to immerse ourselves in and become the other being. We must be able to lose the consciousness which always – in order to remain emotionally healthy – we have to have in the sense world, the consciousness of 'I am myself'. In the elemental world we get to know another being only when in a way we inwardly have 'become' the other. When we have crossed the threshold, we have to move through the elemental world in such a way that with every step we transform ourselves into every single happening, creep into every single being. It belongs to the health of a person's soul that in passing through the sense world he should hold his own and assert his individual character. But this is altogether impossible in the elemental world, where it would lead either to the darkening of his field of vision or to his being thrown back into the sense world.

You will easily understand that in order to exercise the faculty of transformation, the soul needs something more than it already possesses here in our world. The human soul is too weak to be able to change itself continuously and adapt itself to every sort of being if it enters the elemental world in its ordinary state. Therefore the forces of the human soul must be strengthened and heightened through the preparations described in my books *Occult Science* and *Knowledge of Higher Worlds;* from these the life of soul will become stronger and more forceful. It can then immerse itself in other entities without losing itself in the process. This being said, you will understand at once the importance of noting what is called the threshold between the sense world and the supersensible world. We have already said that the clairvoyant consciousness of a human being on earth must go back and forth continually, that it must observe the spiritual world beyond the threshold while it is outside the physical body and must then return into the physical body, exercising in a healthy way the faculties which lead it to the right observation of the physical sense world.

Let us suppose that a person's clairvoyant consciousness,

when returning over the threshold, were to take back into the sense world the faculty of transformation it has to have in order to be at all aware of the spiritual world. The faculty of transformation I have been speaking about is a peculiarity of the human etheric body, which lives by preference in the elemental world. Now suppose that a person were to go back into the physical world keeping his etheric body as capable of transformation as it has to be in the elemental world. What would happen? Each of the worlds has its own special laws. The sense world is the world of self-contained forms, for here the Spirits of Form rule. The elemental world is the world of mobility, of metamorphosis, of transformation; just as we continually have to change in order to feel at home in that world, all the beings there are continually changing themselves. There is no enclosed, circumscribed form: all is in continual metamorphosis. A soul has to take part in this ever-changing existence outside the physical body if it wants to unfold itself there. Then in the physical sense world we must allow our etheric body, as an entity of the elemental world capable of metamorphosis, to sink down into the physical body. Through this physical body I am a definite personality in the physical sense world; I am this or that distinct person. My physical body stamps my personality upon me; the physical body and the conditions of the physical world in which I find myself make me a personality. In the elemental world one is not a personality, for this would require an enclosed form. Here, however, we must note that what the clairvoyant consciousness recognizes in the human soul is, and always has been, present within it. Through the forces of the physical body, the mobility of the etheric body is restrained only for the time being. As soon as the etheric body sinks back into the physical encasement, its powers of movement are held together and adapted to the form. If the etheric body were not tucked into the physical body as if into a tote bag, it would always be impelled to continuous transformation.

Now let us suppose that a soul, becoming clairvoyant, were to carry over into the physical world this desire of its etheric body for transformation. Then with its tendency towards movement it will fit rather loosely into the physical body, and thus the soul can come into contradiction with the physical world that wants to shape it into a definite personality. The etheric body, which always wants to move freely, can come back over the threshold in the wrong way, every moment wishing to be something or someone else, someone that may be quite the opposite of the firmly imprinted form of the physical body. To put it even more concretely: a person could be, say, a Scandinavian bank executive, thanks to his physical body, but because his etheric brings over into the physical world the impulse to free itself from physical constraints he may imagine himself to be the emperor of China. (Or, to use another example, a person may be – let us say – the president of the Theosophical Society, and if her etheric body has been loosened, she may imagine that she has been in the presence of the Director of the Universe.)[40]

We see that the threshold that sharply divides the sense world from the supersensible world must be respected absolutely; the soul must observe the requirements of each of the two worlds, adapting and conducting itself differently on this side and that. We have emphasized repeatedly that the peculiarities of the supersensible world must not unlawfully be carried over when one comes back into the sense world. If I may put it more plainly, one has to understand how to conduct oneself in both worlds; one may not carry over into one world the method of observation that is right for the other.

First of all, then, we have to take note that the essential faculty for finding and feeling oneself in the elemental world is the faculty of transformation. But the human soul could never live permanently in this mobile element. The etheric body could as little remain permanently in a state of being able to transform itself as a human being in the physical world could remain continually awake. Only when we are awake can we observe the physical world; asleep, we do not perceive it. Nevertheless we have to allow the waking condition to alternate with the sleeping one. Something comparable to this is necessary in the elemental world. Just as little as it is right in the physical world to be continually awake, for life here must swing like a pendulum between waking and sleeping, so something similar is necessary for the life of the etheric body in the elemental world. There must be an opposite pole, as it were, something that works in the opposite direction to the faculty of transformation leading to perception in the spiritual world. What is it that makes the human being capable of transformation? It is his living in imagination, in mental images, the ability to make his ideas and thoughts so mobile that through his lively, flexible thinking he can dip down into other beings and happenings. For the opposite condition, comparable to sleep in the sense world, it is the will of the human being that must be developed and strengthened. For the faculty of transformation, thinking or imagination; for the opposite condition, the will.

To understand this, we should consider that in the physical sense world the human being is a self, an ego, an 'I'. It is the physical body, as long as it is awake, that contributes what is necessary for this feeling of self. The forces of the physical body, when the human being sinks down into it, supply him with the power to feel himself an ego, an 'I'. It is different in the elemental world. There the human being himself must achieve to some degree what the physical body achieves in the physical world. He can develop no feeling of self in the elemental world if he does not exert his will, if he himself does not do the 'willing'. This, however, calls for overcoming something that is deeply rooted in us: our love of comfort and convenience. For the elemental world this self-willing is necessary; like the alternation of sleeping and waking in the physical world, the condition of 'transforming oneself into other beings' must give way to the feeling of self-strengthened volition. Just as we have become tired in the physical world and close our eyes, overcome by sleep, the moment comes in the elemental world when the etheric body feels, 'I cannot go on continually changing; now I must shut out all the beings and happenings around me. I will have to thrust it all out of my field of vision and look away from it. I now must will myself and live absolutely and entirely within myself, ignoring the other beings and occurrences.' This willing of self, excluding everything else, corresponds to sleep in the physical world.

We would be mistaken if we imagined that the alternation of transformation with strengthened ego feeling were regulated in the elemental world just as naturally as waking and sleeping are in the physical world. According to clairvoyant consciousness – and to this alone it is perceptible – it takes place at will, not passing so easily as waking here passes into sleep. After one has lived for a time in the element of metamorphosis, one feels the need within oneself to engage and use the other swing of the pendulum of elemental life. In a much more arbitrary way than with our waking and sleeping, the element of transforming oneself alternates with living within with its heightened feeling of self. Yes, our consciousness can even bring it about through its elasticity that in certain circumstances both conditions can be present at the same time: on the one hand, one transforms oneself to some degree and yet can hold together certain parts of the soul and rest within oneself. In the elemental world we can wake and sleep at the same time, something we should not try to do in the physical world if we have any concern for our soul life. We must further consider that when thinking develops into the faculty of transformation and begins to be at home in the elemental world, it cannot be used in that world in the way that is right and healthy for the physical world. What is thinking like in our ordinary world? Observe it as you follow its movement. A person is aware of thoughts in his soul; he knows that he is grasping, spinning out, connecting and separating these thoughts. Inwardly he feels himself to be the master of his thoughts, which seem rather passive; they allow themselves to be connected and separated, to be formed and

178 NATURE SPIRITS

then dismissed. This life of thought must develop in the
elemental world a step further. There a person is not in a
position to deal with thoughts that are passive. If someone
really succeeds in entering that world with his clairvoyant
soul, it seems as though his thoughts were not things over
which he has any command: they are living beings. Only
imagine how it is when you cannot form and connect and
separate your thoughts but, instead, each one of them in your
consciousness begins to have a life of its own, a life as an entity
in itself. You thrust your consciousness into a place, it seems,
where you do not find thoughts that are like those in the
physical world but where they are living beings. I can only use
a grotesque picture which will help us somehow to realize how
different our thinking must become from what it is here.
Imagine sticking your head into an anthill, while your thinking comes to a stop – you would have ants in your head instead
of thoughts! It is just like that, when your soul dips down into
the elemental world; your thoughts become so alive that they
themselves join each other, separate from each other and lead
a life of their own. We truly need a stronger power of soul to
confront these living thought-beings with our consciousness
than we do with the passive thoughts of the physical world,
which allow themselves to be formed at will, to be connected
and separated not only sensibly but often even quite foolishly.
They are patient things, these thoughts of our ordinary world;
they let the human soul do anything it likes with them. But it
is quite different when we thrust our soul into the elemental
world, where our thoughts will lead an independent life. A
human being must hold his own with his soul life and assert
his will in confronting these active, lively, no longer passive
thoughts. In the physical world our thinking can be completely stupid and this does not harm us at all. But if we do
foolish things with our thinking in the elemental world, it may
well happen that our stupid thoughts, creeping around there
as independent beings, can hurt us, can even cause real pain.
    Thus we see that the habits of our soul life must change when

we cross the threshold from the physical into the supersensible world. If we were then to return to the physical world with the activity we have to bring to bear on the living thought entities of the elemental world and failed to develop in ourselves sound thinking with these passive thoughts, wishing rather to hold fast to the conditions of the other world, our thoughts would continually run away from us; then hurrying after them, we would become a slave to our thoughts.

When a person enters the elemental world with clairvoyant soul and develops his faculty of metamorphosis, he delves into it with his inner life, transforming himself according to the kind of entity he is confronting. What is his experience when he does this? It is something we can call sympathy and antipathy. Out of soul depths these experiences seem to well up, presenting themselves to the soul that has become clairvoyant. Quite definite kinds of sympathy and antipathy appear as it transforms itself into this or that other being. When the person proceeds from one transformation to the next, he is continually aware of different sympathies or antipathies. Just as in the physical world we recognize, characterize, describe the objects and living beings, in short, perceive them when the eye sees their colour or the ear hears their tones, so correspondingly in the spiritual world we would describe its beings in terms of particular sympathies and antipathies. Two things, however, should be noted. One is that in our usual way of speaking in the physical world we generally differentiate only between stronger and weaker degrees of sympathy and antipathy; in the elemental world the sympathies and antipathies differ from one another not only in degree but also in *quality*. There they vary, just as yellow here is quite different from red. As our colours are qualitatively different, so are the many varieties of sympathy and antipathy that we meet in the elemental world. In order therefore to describe this correctly, one may not merely say – as one would do in the physical world – that in diving down and entering this particular entity one feels greater sympathy,

while in immersing oneself in another entity one feels less
sympathy. No, sympathies of all sorts and kinds can be found
there.

The other point to note is this. Our usual natural attitude
to sympathy and antipathy cannot be carried over into the
elemental world. Here in this world we feel drawn to some
people, repelled by others; we associate by choice with those
who are sympathetic and wish to stay near them; we turn
away from the things and people who are abhorrent and
refuse to have anything to do with them. This cannot be the
case in the elemental world, for there – if I may express it
rather oddly – we will not find the sympathies sympathetic
nor the antipathies antipathetic. This would resemble someone in the physical world saying, 'I can stand only the blues
and greens, not the red or yellow colours. I simply have to run
away from red and yellow!' If a being of the elemental world
is antipathetic, it means that it has a distinct characteristic of
that world which must be described as antipathetic, and we
have to deal with it just as we deal in the sense world with the
colours blue and red – not permitting one to be more
sympathetic to us than the other. Here we meet all the colours
with a certain calmness because they convey what the things
are; only when a person is a bit neurotic does he run away
from certain colours, or when he is a bull and cannot bear the
sight of red. Most of us accept all the colours with equanimity
and in the same way we should be able to observe with the
utmost calmness the qualities of sympathy and antipathy that
belong to the elemental world. For this we must necessarily
change the attitude of soul usual in the physical world, where
it is attracted by sympathy and repelled by antipathy; it must
become completely changed. There the inner mood or disposition corresponding to the feelings of sympathy and antipathy
must be replaced with what we can call soul-quiet, spirit-
peacefulness.[41] With an inwardly resolute soul life filled with
spirit calm, we must immerse ourselves in the entities and
transform ourselves into them; then we will feel the qualities

of these beings rising within our soul depths as sympathies and antipathies. Only when we can do this, with such an attitude toward sympathy and antipathy, will the soul, in its experiences, be capable of letting the sympathetic and antipathetic perception appear before it as images that are right and true. That is, only then are we capable not merely of feeling what the perception of sympathies and antipathies is but of really experiencing our own particular self, transformed into another being, suddenly rising up as one or another colour-picture or as one or another tone-picture of the elemental world.

You can also learn how sympathies and antipathies play a part in regard to the experience of the soul in the spiritual world if you will look with a certain amount of inner understanding at the chapter of my book *Theosophy* that describes the soul world. You will see there that the soul world is actually constructed of sympathies and antipathies. From my description you will have been able to learn that what we know as thinking in the physical sense world is really only the external shadowy imprint, called up by the physical body, of the thinking that, lying in occult depths, can be called a true living force. As soon as we enter the elemental world and move with our etheric body, thoughts become – one can say – denser, more alive, more independent, more true to their own nature. What we experience as thought in the physical body relates to this truer element of thinking as a shadow on the wall relates to the objects casting it. As a matter of fact, it is the shadow of the elemental thought-life thrown into the physical sense world through the instrumentality of the physical body. When we think, our thinking lies more or less in the shadow of thought beings. Here clairvoyant spiritual knowledge throws new light on the true nature of thinking. No philosophy, no external science, however ingenious, can determine anything of the real nature of thinking; only a knowledge based on clairvoyant consciousness can recognize what it is.

The same thing holds good with the nature of our willing. The will must grow stronger, for in the elemental world things are not so obliging that the ego feeling is provided for us as it is through the forces of the physical body. There we ourselves have to will the feeling of ego; we have to find out what it means for our soul to be entirely filled with the consciousness,' I will myself'; we have to experience something of the greatest significance: that when we are not strong enough to bring forth the real act of will, 'I will myself', and not just the thought of it, at that moment we will feel ourselves falling unconscious as though in a faint. If we do not hold ourselves together in the elemental world, we will fall into a kind of faint. There we look into the true nature of the will, again something that cannot be discovered by external science or philosophy but only by the clairvoyant consciousness. What we call the will in the physical world is a shadowy image of the strong, living will of the elemental world, which grows and develops so that it can maintain the self out of its own volition without the support of external forces. We can say that everything in that world, when we grow accustomed to it, becomes self-willed.

Above all, when we have left the physical body and our etheric body has the elemental world as its environment, it is through the innate character of the etheric body that the drive to transform ourselves awakens. We wish to immerse ourselves in the other beings. However, just as in our waking state by day the need for sleep arises, so in the elemental world there arises in turn the need to be alone, to shut out everything into which we could transform ourselves. Then again, when we have felt alone for a while and developed the strong feeling of will, 'I will myself', there comes what may be called a terrible feeling of isolation, of being forsaken, which evokes the longing to awaken out of this state, of only willing oneself, to the faculty of transformation again. While we rest in physical sleep, other forces take care that we wake up; we do not have to attend to it ourselves. In the elemental world when we are in the sleeping condition of only willing ourselves, it is through the demand of feeling forsaken that we are impelled to put ourselves into the state of transformation, that is, of wanting to awaken.

From all this, you see how different are the conditions of experiencing oneself in the elemental world, of perceiving oneself there, from those of the physical world. You can judge therefore how necessary it is, again and again, to take care that the clairvoyant consciousness, passing back and forth from one world to the other, adapts itself correctly to the requirements of each world and does not carry over, on crossing the threshold, the usages of one into the other. The strengthening and invigorating of the life of soul consequently belongs to the preparation we have often described as necessary for the experience of supersensible worlds.

What must above all become strong and forceful are the soul experiences we can call the eminently moral ones. These imprint themselves as soul dispositions in firmness of character and inner resolute calm. Inner courage and firmness of character must most especially be developed, for through weakness of character we cripple the whole life of soul, which would then come powerless into the elemental world; this we must avoid if we hope to have a true and correct experience there. No one who is really earnest about gaining knowledge in the higher worlds will therefore fail to give weight to the strengthening of the *moral* forces among all the other forces that help the soul enter those worlds. One of the most shameful errors is foisted on humanity when someone takes it on himself to say that clairvoyance should be acquired without paying attention to strengthening the moral life. It must be stressed once and for all that what I described in my book *Knowledge of Higher Worlds* as the development of the lotus flowers that crystallize in the spirit body of a student-clairvoyant may indeed take place without attention to supportive moral strength, but certainly ought not to do so.

The lotus flowers must be there if a person wants to have the faculty of transformation. That faculty comes into existence when the flowers unfold their petals in a motion away from the human being, in order to grasp the spiritual world and adhere to it. Whatever a person develops as the ability to transform himself is expressed for the clairvoyant vision in the unfolding of the lotus flowers. Whatever he can acquire of a strengthened ego-feeling becomes inner firmness; we can call it an elementary backbone. Both of these must be correspondingly developed: the lotus flowers so that one can transform oneself, and an elementary backbone so that one can unfold a strengthened ego in the elemental world.

As mentioned in an earlier lecture, what develops in a spiritual way can lead to a high order of virtues in the spiritual world. But if this is allowed to stream down into the sense world, it can bring about the most terrible vices. It is the same with the lotus flowers and elemental backbone. By practising certain methods it is also possible to awaken the lotus flowers and backbone without aiming for moral firmness – but this no conscientious clairvoyant would recommend. It is not merely a question of attaining something or other in the higher worlds, but of knowing what is involved. At the moment we pass over the threshold into the spiritual world we approach the luciferic and ahrimanic beings, of whom we have already spoken; here we meet them in quite a different way from any confrontation we might have in the physical world. We will have the remarkable experience that as soon as we cross the threshold, that is, as soon as we have developed the lotus flowers and a backbone, we will see the luciferic powers coming towards us with the intention of seizing the lotus flowers. They stretch their tentacles out towards our lotus flowers; we must have developed in the right way so that we use the lotus flowers to grasp and understand the spiritual events and so that they are not themselves grasped by the luciferic powers. It is possible to prevent their being seized by these powers only by ascending into the spiritual world with firmly established moral forces.

I have already mentioned that in the physical sense world the ahrimanic forces approach us more from outside, the luciferic more from within the soul. In the spiritual world it is just the opposite: the luciferic beings come from outside and try to lay hold of the lotus flowers, whereas the ahrimanic beings come from within and settle themselves tenaciously within the elementary backbone. If we have risen into the spiritual world without the support of morality, the ahrimanic and luciferic powers form an extraordinary alliance with each other. If we have come into the higher worlds filled with ambition, vanity, pride or with the desire for power, Ahriman and Lucifer will succeed in forming a partnership with each other. I will use a picture for what they do, but this picture corresponds to the actual situation and you will understand that what I am indicating really takes place. Ahriman and Lucifer form an alliance; together they bind the petals of the lotus flowers to the elementary backbone. When all the petals are fastened to the backbone, the human being is tied up in himself, fettered within himself through his strongly developed lotus flowers and backbone. The results of this will be the onset of egoism and love of deception to an extent that would be impossible were he to remain normally in the physical world. Thus we see what can happen if clairvoyant consciousness is not developed in the right way: the alliance of Ahriman and Lucifer whereby the petals of the lotus flowers are fastened onto the elementary backbone, fettering a person within himself by means of his own elemental or etheric capacities. These are the things we must know if we wish to penetrate with open eyes and with understanding into the actual spiritual world.

Sources of the lectures by Rudolf Steiner

'Elemental Beings of Earth and Water', 3 April 1912, and 'Elemental Beings and the Spirits of the Cosmos', 4 April 1912, are from *Spiritual Beings in the Heavenly Bodies and in the Kingdoms of Nature* (GA136), published by Anthroposophic Press, 1992.

'Redemption of the Elementals by the Human Being', 12 April 1909, is included in *The Spiritual Hierarchies and Their Reflection in the Physical World* (GA110), published by Anthroposophic Press, 1970.

'Gnomes, Undines, Sylphs and Salamanders', 16 May 1908, and 'Phantoms, Spectres and Demons', 4 June 1908, are included in *The Influence of Spiritual Beings on Man* (from GA102), published by Anthroposophic Press, 1961.

'Elemental Spirits of Birth and Death', 6 October 1917, is included in *The Fall of the Spirits of Darkness* (GA177), published by Rudolf Steiner Press, 1993.

'Truth, Beauty, Goodness and the Elemental Beings', 16 December 1922, is included in *Man and the World of Stars* (GA219), published by Anthroposophic Press, 1963.

'Elemental Spirits and the Plant World', 2 November 1923 and 'Elemental Spirits and the Animal Kingdom', 3 November 1923, are included in *Man as Symphony of the Creative Word* (GA230), published by Rudolf Steiner Press, 1991.

'Ahrimanic Elemental Beings', 19 August 1924, is included in *True and False Paths in Spiritual Investigation* (GA243), published by Rudolf Steiner Press, 1985.

'The Elemental World and the Future of Mankind', 28 May 1922, is taken from *The Human Soul in Relation to World Evolution* (GA212), published by the Anthroposophic Press, 1985.

'Perception of the Elemental World', 26 August 1913, is taken from *Secrets of the Threshold* (GA147), published by Anthroposophic Press, 1987.

All the above works are available from Rudolf Steiner Press (UK) or Anthroposophic Press (USA).

Notes

GA = *Gesamtausgabe*, the collected edition of Rudolf Steiner's works in the original German (published by Rudolf Steiner Verlag, Dornach, Switzerland).
RSP = Rudolf Steiner Press, London
AP = Anthroposophic Press, New York.

1. Quoted from *Denken im Gespräch mit dem Engel* by Wolf-Ulrich Klünker, Stuttgart 1988, page 98.
2. This and the following quotes are taken from Rudolf Steiner's lecture of 12 April 1909 (evening), GA110; in this volume the lecture appears on page 46.
3. *The Soul's Awakening* by Rudolf Steiner, in: *Four Mystery Plays*, GA14, RSP, 1982.
4. *Ibid.*
5. *Ibid.*
6. *Ibid.*
7. This and the following quotes are taken from Rudolf Steiner's lecture of 26 August 1913 (GA147). In this volume the lecture appears on page 171.
8. Quoted from Erigena by Klünker, page 88.
9. *Periphyseon* by Johannes Scotus Erigena, (Dublin, 1968). Latin text: Migne, Patrologia Latina 122, col. 441 A.
10. *Ibid.* part 1, Migne PL 122, col. 441 B.
11. Lecture by Rudolf Steiner of 14 November 1923 (GA228), not translated.
12. See, for example, *Periphyseon*, part 2. Migne PL 122, col. 876.
13. *Ibid.* Migne PL 122, col. 879 B.
14. *Ibid.* Migne PL 122, col. 896 D.
15. *Ibid.* Migne PL 122, col. 950 AB.
16. Lecture by Rudolf Steiner of 16 September 1923 (GA228), not translated.
17. See the following lectures:
    27 December 1923, 29 December 1923 (GA223), *World History in the Light of Anthroposophy*, RSP, 1977. 4 January 1924, 5 January 1924, 12 January 1924 (GA233a),

Rosicrucianism and Modern Initiation, RSP, 1965. 31 March 1924 (GA239), *Karmic Relationships*, Vol. V, RSP, 1966. 1 July 1924, 13 July 1924, 1 August 1924 (GA237), *Karmic Relationships*, Vol. VIII, RSP, 1977. 14 August 1924 (GA240), *Karmic Relationships*, Vol. VI, RSP, 1971. 12 September 1924 (GA238), *Karmic Relationships*, Vol. IV, RSP, 1957.

18. *Anthroposophical Leading Thoughts* by Rudolf Steiner (GA26), RSP, 1973.

19. *Ibid.*: 'From Nature to Sub-nature'.

20. The teachers who guided the people of Ancient India. See *Occult Science: An Outline*, RSP, 1969.

21. Gospel of St. John, chapter 8, verse 32: 'And ye shall know the truth and the truth shall make you free.'

22. Heinrich von Ferstel, 1828–83, designer of the votive church in Vienna. See also: *Rudolf Steiner, Studien zu seinem Lebensgang und Lebenswerk* by Emil Bock, Stuttgart 1967, page 41.

23. Acts of the Apostles, chapter 2, verse 3.

24. Leonardo da Vinci, 1452–1519.

25. Examples are the chapter on the evolution of the world and the human being in *Occult Science: An Outline*, and the chapter on our Atlantean forebears in *Cosmic Memory*, Steinerbooks, New York, 1976.

26. Ricarda Huch (1864–1947), German writer: *Luthers Glaube, Briefe an einen Freund* (Luther's faith, letters to a friend), Leipzig: Insel-Verlag 1916. A new edition of the work appeared in 1964.

27. Quote from Goethe's *Faust*, Part 1, scene in Auerbach's Tavern.

28. Matthew 18:20.

29. The German term for 'tawny beast' is 'blonde Bestie'. Nietzsche experts are in two minds about the interpretation of the term. It comes from Nietzsche's *Zur Genealogie der Moral* (1887, I, 11): 'das Raubtier, die prachtvolle nach Beute lüstern schweifende blonde Bestie' (the predator, that magnificent blonde/tawny beast roaming far and wide lusting for prey). One interpretation is that this refers to the Janissary, a 'killing order' of warriors who in their boyhood

had been taken from Christian families by the Turks and thus removed from the humanizing influence of a family, trained to be utterly ruthless and inhuman. Other experts, and clearly also Ricarda Huch, think the term refers to a lion. (Translator.)

30. The struggle for dominion over human nature between luciferic and ahrimanic beings is also described in the three London lectures of 12, 16 and 19 November 1922, in *Man's Life on Earth and in the Spiritual Worlds*, Anthroposophical Publishing Co., London, 1952, GA218.

31. *The Soul's Awakening* by Rudolf Steiner; 2nd scene of the fourth Mystery Drama, GA14 (see note 3).

32. Imagination, Inspiration and Intuition are three perceptive faculties achieved as part of the anthroposophic path of knowledge. Rudolf Steiner described these and ways of achieving them on many occasions. See his *Occult Science: An Outline*. A clear exposition is also given in his *Fruits of Anthroposophy*, RSP 1986.

33. In *Wahrheit aus Jean Pauls Leben. Kindheitsgeschichte von ihm selbst geschrieben*, Breslau 1826–28, 1st volume, page 53.

34. See Rudolf Steiner's *The Soul's Awakening*, second scene: gnome-spirits' chorus, sylph-spirits' chorus.

35. A structure at the heart of the flower, consisting of the ovary containing the ovules and the style bearing the stigma. In botanical works usually referred to as 'the female reproductive organ of flowering plants'. (Translator.)

36. In *Goethes Naturwissenschaftlichen Schriften*, 5th volume, edited with a commentary by Rudolf Steiner 1884–97 in Kürschner's *Deutsche National-Literatur*, GA1 a–e, Dornach 1975, volume 1, page 163.

37. Goethe jotted down the words: 'Study dispersal as dust, evaporation, dispersal in droplets'. See Rudolf Steiner's 'Goethe the Scientist' in *Goethean Science*, Mercury Press, New York, 1988.

38. Rudolf Steiner, *On the Life of the Soul*, AP, 1985.

39. In *Der Goetheanumgedanke inmitten der Kulturkrisis der Gegenwart. Gesammelte Aufsätze aus der Wochenschrift 'Das Goetheanum'*, 1921–25, GA36.

40. Leadbeater wrote that he had 'stood with Mrs Besant in the presence of the Director of the Universe'. Mrs Besant was at that time the President of the Theosophical Society.

41. See *The Soul's Awakening*, Scene 4. The Guardian of the Threshold says:

> You see myself, too, in delusion's form
> while vain desires are joined to inner sight
> and spirit peacefulness as sheath of soul
> has not yet taken hold of your whole being.

Rudolf Steiner
Self-Transformation
Selected Lectures

At the heart of Rudolf Steiner's spiritual philosophy is the
path of inner development leading to personal
transformation. Steiner shows how, through specific
meditative exercises, it is possible to break out of the restricted
world of everyday consciousness. He gives advice on the
development of inner qualities such as clear thinking, inner
tranquillity and positivity, which lay a necessary foundation
for esoteric work.

In contrast to many of the New Age paths available today,
Steiner's methods are based on the Western tradition, the
Rosicrucian path of initiation, as opposed to older Eastern
teachings. This modern way, he suggests, is a metamorphosis
of the Eastern paths and is best suited to modern
consciousness. Speaking as an initiate, he describes the levels
of attainment on this spiritual journey, the first being
'imagination' where the spiritual world is revealed in pictures,
followed by 'inspiration' and finally 'intuition'.

ISBN 1 855840 19 7; 256pp; £12.95

Rudolf Steiner
Evil
Selected Lectures

Despite the fact that evil is an omnipresent theme of our age, it remains one of the most problematic. Public references to it are continually made, but to what extent has society truly begun to understand its riddle?

In this selection of insightful lectures Rudolf Steiner addresses the subject of evil from the results of his spiritual research, offering an original and complex picture. He describes evil as a phenomenon which arises when a thing appears outside its true context, enabling something which is initially 'good' to become harmful. He speaks of the effect of particular spiritual beings—principally Lucifer and Ahriman—who work as polar forces, laying hindrances in our path. Yet, paradoxically, confronting and coming to terms with such difficulties ultimately furthers our development. Thus Steiner speaks of evil as a necessary phenomenon in human evolution, allowing for the possibility of freedom.

ISBN 1 855840 46 4; 224pp; £11.95

Rudolf Steiner
Life Beyond Death
Selected Lectures

Although western humanity has conquered the outer world
with the aid of technology and science, death remains an
unsolved and largely unexplored mystery. Rudolf Steiner, an
exceptional seer, was able to research spiritually the question
of what happens to human consciousness after the physical
body passes away. In these remarkably matter-of-fact lectures
he affirms that life continues beyond death. Far from being
dissipated, the individual's consciousness awakens to a new
reality, beginning a great journey to the farthest expanses of
the cosmos. Here it embarks on a process of purification and
preparation.

Rudolf Steiner indicates that one of the most important tasks
for our present civilization is the reestablishment of living
connections with those who have died. He gives suggestions
as to how this can be done safely, and describes how the dead
can be of help to those on earth.

ISBN 1 855840 17 0; 256pp; £12.95

Rudolf Steiner
Angels
Selected Lectures

Religious and spiritual writings have always made reference to
beings from the spiritual hierarchies, especially those known
in Christian tradition as Angels. These spirits are the closest
to human beings and act as our invisible guides and
companions. They influence the life of the individual as well
as the evolution of humanity and the cosmos.

From his own clairvoyant vision Rudolf Steiner confirmed the
existence of such spiritual beings, and showed how modern
minds could gain access to their world. As he explains in these
inspiring lectures, it is important for us to understand and
cooperate with the work of the Angels today as this is crucial
for the further development of humanity.

ISBN 1 855840 60 X; 192pp; £10.95